A Leader Like You

Harnessing Your Leadership Superpower As A Christian Career Professional

By

Dr. Marcia Thomas

Table of Contents

Chapter 3

Chapter 4

Chapter 5

Chapter 6

Dedication

This book is dedicated to the most precious gifts in my life after my number one Sustainer, Master Servant Leader, Strong Tower, Shield and Defense, Deliverer, Keeper, Savior and Friend --- my two children, Kharl and Helen, my son-in-law Damar and my granddaughter Adalia.

No one will ever understand how much you sacrifice in allowing me to serve others.

Thank you for your tireless support. I thank God for the strong leaders you are and am proud of your dedication to duty, family and community.

Acknowledgements

So many people have inspired and continue to inspire me to be God's best that I could never mention everyone by name.

I sincerely thank my mother for being my greatest role model for introducing me to Christ before I was born, growing me up in Christ and being my prayer partner.

Thank you, my dear sisters Carole, Yolande and Sandra, adopted sisters, Annecha, Christine, Claudine, Janice, and Sophia for believing in me and being my ultimate source of strength.

Thank you, Locksley, for being my steady, immovable and silent support and my ultimate sounding board.

Thank you, Clive, for giving your time, wisdom, divine inspiration and being a faith battery for this product.

To all my tribe that I call and know to be my friends and who know themselves. You have stood by me in thick and thin. You have helped me learn to put in practice many of the lessons in this book. Mochas gracias!

I have a deep and abiding love for you all.

Introduction

The Power of Leadership Reflection

Facing a group of curious nine-year-old's in my Sabbath school class, I hesitated but brimmed with excitement to share Jonah's tale of disobedience and surrender. With a deep breath, I began the captivating journey of storytelling, hoping to leave a lasting impression on their tender hearts.

How did I get here? Everyone had received the same vision. Everyone had the same prophecy. 'You are a born leader.'

At the tender age of nine, my upbringing in the church weighed heavily on me. My mother held studying the Sabbath school junior quarterly and memorizing the required lesson texts on Thirteen Sabbath as sacred tasks. To forget or falter in these duties felt like an unpardonable sin, and the pressure to meet her expectations was a constant burden on my young shoulders.

In all honesty, my generation, including my family, particularly my mother, were deeply committed church members. They enjoyed the affirmations, accolades, commendations, and treats I received from being the unbeatable champion.

However, I had one issue. My vivacious, argumentative, exuberant spirit and my uncultured habit of asking awkward questions disturbed the established status quo.

Therefore, the Christian thing to do was to reward me that coveted place. It was a way to reinforce my commitment to church activities and ensure that I remained dedicated, all while potentially curbing any future tendencies to disrupt the peace or stray from the path they deemed appropriate.

The Journey to Becoming a Leader

Over forty years ago, I was chosen by default for instruction and training in my Sabbath school class, like Jonah. Of course, that wasn't enough to suppress my 'unruly disposition,' and so I was assigned a Christian leadership mentor with a proven track record of success to teach me the rudiments of youth leadership and show me by example how to teach, empower, mentor and model 'Christ-like' characters among my peers.

Looking back, I realize that the mission to 'curb me' orchestrated by well-intentioned church leaders was divinely guided, solidifying my belief in God's divine orchestration of a righteous person's steps.

Despite my initial resistance to the pressure placed upon me by my devoted Christian mother, who has been a steadfast role model in her faith, I eventually embraced the teachings and values she imparted.

This enhanced my effectiveness as a leader for life. I matriculated wonderfully and graduated with an honors diploma in 'mission responsibility.'

I embraced a personal mantra or philosophy of leadership that remains my constant guide as an advocate, supporter, enabler, enforcer, mentor, and coach.

'To thine own self be true thou canst not then be false to any man' (Hamlet 8)

This philosophy finds its roots in what I believe to be the most timeless and relevant leadership quote ever penned by a devoted servant of God and a fully surrendered Christian leader back in 1844.

This quote sheds light on what I call the "new leadership pandemic" - the presence of a lack of integrity masked under the guise of insightful or strong leadership.

'The greatest want of the world is

the want of men—men who will not be bought or sold; men who in their inmost souls are true and honest; men who do not fear to call sin by its right name; men whose conscience is as true to duty as the needle to the pole; men who will stand for the right though the heavens fall" (White, 2007)

With these weapons of awareness and greater clarity, I excelled as a class rep, Sabbath schoolteacher, youth leader, district youth representative, youth board member, and student council representative. So, as a Christian leader, I was armed and divinely dangerous.

Chapter 1

Humble Follower, Confident Leader

"Since we have gifts that differ according to the grace given to us, each of us is to use them accordingly: if [someone has the gift of] prophecy, [let him speak a new message from God to His people] in proportion to the faith possessed; if service, in the act of serving; or he who teaches, in the act of teaching; or he who encourages, in the act of encouragement; he who gives, with generosity; he who leads, with diligence; he who shows mercy [in caring for others], with cheerfulness." **Romans 12:6-8**

In 1989, my intensive leadership journey began, and since then, it has been a long and diverse road.

It has taken me down many different paths, spanning from class teacher, senior teacher, department head, staff rep, Vice Chairperson, principal, coach, trainer, and consultant.

As I reflect on my journey from follower to confident servant leader, I have faced my share of ups and downs, curveballs, and bumps.

Over the past twelve years as an instructional leader, trainer, and coach, I have gained profound insights into the essence of leadership. I know what it means to have your faith tested and tried. Most importantly, I have accepted that for a Christian leader in a professional space, our crucibles originate from a spiritual battlefield. We are in spiritual warfare.

Through introspective reflections, I have honed a remarkable, insightful, and genuine ability to recognize the weapons and subtle tactics employed by the enemy when launching attacks against Christian leaders.

I have learned how to:

☒ Fight discouragement (personal and professional).

☒ Accept betrayals from people I had misjudged as friends.

☒ Handle pressure (personal and professional).

☒ Persevere despite leadership misfortune, traumas, loss, stress, confrontation, and conflict.

☒ Overlook intentional and unintentional offense

☒ Manage time effectively while trying to cater to the needs of various individuals

☒ Ignore distractions from wolves in sheep's clothing.

☒ Endure insensitive, unfair, and unreasonable requests and comments.

☒ Successfully wade through misunderstandings.

☒ Acknowledge leadership paralysis and leadership loneliness.

☒ Hug my tears and sorrows.

☒ Juggle death, oppression, repression and illness.

As I faced numerous challenging situations with minimal support and without being rescued, understood, or defended, I learned to toughen up and rely on my inner strength. I became an executive leader of resilience.

Thank God, I have grown and matured by His grace and enabling.

To be honest, this journey of growth was far from easy. I can vividly recall the day I first visited the organization where I have served as an instructional leader and a Christian for twelve years.

I attended my interview, and I emerged as the most convincing candidate out of twelve applicants. I was ecstatic, fearless, energized, engaged, and driven. I was so determined to make a difference.

My contract was signed and sealed, and my provisional appointment was approaching the final stages. I was excited, motivated, and fully committed to excel on this leg of my journey. I had God's approval and the support of my family. At the height of all this, I also got favorable responses from two larger institutions where I had been rigorously interviewed. I had a huge dilemma. I questioned God. *'Why now and not before? What should I do?' Could this be a counterfeit assignment?*

After seeking guidance from the heavenly host and receiving confirmation from numerous established experts in the field, I was convinced I had found the answer. With unwavering certainty, I settled into my position without hesitation.

My Leadership Pathway

There is a saying, 'see me and come live with me, two different things. This became my reality. So many things needed to be done. So many empty promises of support and mentorship from people I had given my trust and confidence.

Many of the supposedly foolproof principles of delegation, motivation, collaboration, and stakeholder participation that I formally learned for effective leadership fell short of their touted promises, as they often mirrored others' thoughts rather than offering unique insights.

As time passed, I came to realize that the technocrats believed in the notion that a "one- size-fits-all" approach could work if skillfully adjusted to deceive those who were unaware. The repeated assurances and perpetual frustration stemming from unfulfilled promises made it clear that they were completely sold out to this idea.

The organization I was appointed to lead is dumbed a small remote rural school. At the time of my appointment, it had three hundred and ninety-six students and nine teachers, one canteen cooks, and an aged grounds man. It had a modern teachers' bathroom, the handiwork of the previous principal, no staff room, a small room to facilitate the principal, a makeshift library and a small canteen in dire need of repair, and a pit latrine bathroom facility for the students.

There were major infrastructural factors that were glaring. For example, the institution was:

☒ Located in a deprived area.
☒ Located far from the nearest police station, hospital, and public library.
☒ Has no telephone, improper water systems (depends on rainfall/water truck), and outdated electrical wiring.
☒ Limited funding mechanisms.
☒ Insufficient government grants and allocations.
☒ Severe deficiencies in school infrastructure.
☒ Lack of school library.
☒ Lack well needed educational resources (textbooks, multimedia projector, science equipment) and the proper infrastructure to maximize teaching and learning via technology.
☒ Principal often responsible for extensive administrative, supervisory, extracurricular, and maintenance responsibilities as a classroom teacher.

There were also some classroom and socio-cultural factors that I cannot avoid highlighting.

Classroom Factors:

☒ Classes were overcrowded.
☒ Some classrooms had chalkboard partitions.
☒ Limited classroom space.
☒ Small enrollment.
☒ Students and teachers have limited or no access to technology and other media services.
☒ Teachers engaged students with additional needs.
☒ Teachers lacked training in multigrid instruction.

- Teachers had multiple extracurricular duties.
- Teachers had to constantly increase planning and material preparation for instruction.

Socio-Cultural Factors

- No telephone.
- No running waters.
- Most students walked to school.
- Weak social networks and resources to promote early learning.
- Police station, hospital and commercial services were30km away.
- Lack of support for parents dealing with special needs children.
- Low-income families (farmers).
- Lack of/inadequate parent and community involvement.
- Inadequate supervision and support from local authorities (School board, Ministry of education), parents and community.

This government-owned institution received an annual maintenance grant of $30,000 that increased post-COVID to a whopping $150,000. The most pressing leadership challenge was the total of my 'leadership inheritance', which include limited human, financial, material, and technical resources. I received an unexpected bonus: the people I was now to lead but did not choose. They were packaged, labeled, and delivered. 'You either make them or break them', was the insightful remark from a key stakeholder.

The teachers arrived with high expectations but

showed a passive-aggressive resistance to change. The parents brought their free-spirited nature, entrenched norms, rebellious habits, and a strong clan structure. Additionally, the students' underperformance on standardized tests added to the challenges I faced.

The community in which the institution was embedded contained members who were unbridled in their passions and more concerned with their day-to-day survival rather than the children's education. If you wanted to have a well-attended productive PTA meeting, school leaving exercise, sports day, seminar, workshop, or community program, it would have to be ideally set for a Monday or Tuesday.

Wednesdays to Saturdays were market days for most parents who were both farmers and hagglers.

These complex factors presented numerous dilemmas. I soon discovered that what was in the showcase was definitely not in the stock room and that the technocrats were miserable comforters, i.e., experts in removing cobwebs rather than killing the spider. The magnitude of this realization was such that I found myself going through a profound grieving process.

I went from shock to denial to depression and gradually settled into an acceptance that mushroomed into a bargaining mode.

Three years into my leadership journey, the battle lines were drawn. I finally accepted that you could thrive as a leader as long as you obey the unwritten rules of 'engagement, empowerment and accountability', - 'do as I say and not as I do' and recognize and remain where your superiors decide to position you on the leadership stage based on round table criteria.

In this specific stakeholder context, effective or successful leadership hinges on one's ability to excel in a multitude of roles. This includes mastering the art of being a data entry clerk, a one-day seminar-trained accountant, a subconscious enforcer, a TEO virtual assistant, a security guard, a maintenance officer, an outstanding 'solopreneur,' a call center agent, a doctor, a nurse, a lawyer, an unpaid political aid, and a docile recipient of preferential handouts. Juggling these diverse responsibilities is crucial for achieving leadership success within this complex environment.

You are most certainly the affirmed life changing, flexible change agent first, if you perfect the art of responding to unreasonable demands at odd hours of the night. Second, if you measure up and commit to unrealistic goals that even the blind can see will not be met by the incredulous deadline. Third, how convincingly you sacrifice health and home to maintain the numerous smokescreens of progress, productivity, and performance.

You are strategic and exceptional when you prove you have the dexterity to carry water in the designated baskets. Another exceptional leadership trait points to how grateful you are and how you demonstrate your appreciation when after pleading and begging the technocrats for support in crucial areas, you discover three to five years later that you are tenth on a list.

In a somewhat nonchalant manner, the power

brokers inform you to pray and keep your fingers crossed, as the selection process for the next opportunity is uncertain and hopeful. Their guidance comes with an air of unpredictability, leaving you to rely on faith and chance for a potential future opportunity.

You can surely reach the pinnacle of success when you are able to squeeze the life out of your meager resources without depleting them; Or by how often you choose to remain oblivious to these hidden truths, and how well you train and command your team members to suffer in silence and always look at the bright side. I had to make a choice very early.

The undeniable fact is that you can choose to be an idealistic optimist or a realistic enthusiast. In other words, you can operate from a place of realistic often unnerving and authentic serving (significance) or a place of half-truths, fear, hope, blind submission, and false success. I chose the former. You can seek either success or significance. Zig Ziglar eloquently states that 'God call us not to be successful but to be significant. When we focus on significance, success is usually part of the package'

Based on the unwritten rules of engagement, empowerment, and accountability, successful means that I would be a leader who:

☒ Enforce rather than enable

☒ Deprive rather than entrust

☒ Command rather than connect

☒ Compete rather than cooperate
☒ Controlling rather than compassionate

Exacting and demanding rather than open and genuine

☒ Tolerant rather than loving unconditionally
☒ Exclude rather than include

Of course, there is nothing wrong with aspiring to be an example and striving to perform at your best. Excelling and standing out are admirable desires and aiming for the pinnacle of your career is a worthy goal. As much as possible, you should:

☒ Meet every deadline
☒ Have a high self esteem
☒ Take pride in what you do
☒ Set and maintain high standards
☒ Set goals and work towards accomplishing them
☒ Always have an 'A' game and a plan 'B'
☒ Be an expert in your field or industry
☒ Be a perfect model of excellence
☒ Be persistent and resilient

These are traits of a highly effective leader. However, when your leadership motive is to acquire these traits at the expense of others, merely to win, you can never be successful. You are a winner, yes, but your efforts have little or no significance.

To achieve the paradigm shift from success to significance, I needed patience, consistency, determination, and strong willpower. However, the journey was arduous, involving changing mindsets, reframing structures, challenging norms, and forging partnerships with stakeholders. Building capacity and implementing targeted actions added to the challenges.

No matter what you hear about leadership, types, roles, effectiveness, success, or significance, one thing is certain; leadership rests on two pillars. You – the leader and your team – those you lead. You and your team are all human. Each member of your team is unique.

Each member has a motivation language. Each member has an unwritten agenda. Each has their own baggage and belonging perspective.

The personal baggage, belonging, perspective, or unwritten agenda, remain hidden until they get angry or frustrated.

Similarly, every leader has motives, baggage, an agenda, and a belonging language. Your experiences on your journey carry a beat and a rhythm. As you press into your position and persevere into your purpose, you identify the tune.

Defining Moments of Leadership

Sorin made (2017) posits that defining moments define your leadership. As I emerged as a leader, I can confidently say that I encountered numerous defining moments that shaped my journey.

I distinctly remember the first day I started my journey as a Christian leader in this professional space (educational institution). Of course, it was a Monday, the first workday of every week for most people. I had several defining moments in just one day.

During my "getting to know you" session, the initial meeting with my team, I encountered a self-appointed leader from the inherited team. This person presented me with a list of dos and don'ts that the team had compiled, aiming to facilitate a smooth transition.

At that crucial moment, I astutely observed the team's facial expressions and body language, which conveyed a mix of emotions: disgust, pursed lips, apprehension, cynicism, a sense of "not again," and an attitude of "let us see what will happen." These cues guided my response and approach to the situation.

Looking back, I can smile because to this day I am still grateful for that defining moment. If my memory serves me right, it was a defining leadership moment for my team. I was not prepared to make any pressure point decisions and that message was calmly, but decisively communicated with the following reasons.

I was just settling into the position and needed to find my bearings.

I needed to be given the time to identify and clearly define my why and understand my leadership assignment.

Of course, it is never wise for a leader to ignore the pain points of their team. Therefore, in my quiet time, I painstakingly scrutinized each item using emotional intelligence. I engaged each member of the team separately and individually based on the 'heart throbs 'on the list I received. I asked meaningful and focused questions and listened to every answer without judgment.

This method served me well. In a short time, I discovered that most of the dos and don'ts on the list were personal requests from a disgruntled team player, who had hoped to become the institution's leader because not only was it his alma mater, he also felt that it was merited because of his years of service and informal mentorship by the former leader. Time would now be the master. I knew that it would take a natural cohesion based on performance and trust to convert him and secure his commitment and loyalty. After all the proof of the pudding is in the eating.

In that very moment, my mindset got a new room. I made the decision to focus on changing the physical aspects within my control while also accepting the things I could not change immediately. Recognizing the importance of shifting my team's mindset, I took cohesive and gradual steps toward achieving that goal.

As a leader, it is never wise to allow anyone or anything to pressure you into deciding. Haste is always waste and making a permanent decision on a temporary emotion can negatively alter the desired outcome. The key is to respond and not react. There were other such defining moments. I maneuvered my way through:

- Communication hurdles
- Subjective stakeholders, peers and staff
- Conflict, and confrontational situations
- Performance highs and lows
- Standardized tests
- Meeting expectations, and other situations
- Pain
- Criticism
- Misunderstandings
- Leadership aloneness and loneliness
- Exclusiveness
- Marginalization
- Trauma
- Desperation and loss

As I journeyed through these vibrant scenes of leadership, I share my story because it has taught me invaluable lessons about human dynamics, leadership, Christian leadership, self- awareness, emotional intelligence and self- discovery. Despite facing challenging and even devastating circumstances, I have learned to persevere and not lose hope, emerging stronger and more resilient along the way.

Most importantly, I have confronted and discovered myself on my journey of becoming a significant leader. I can never underestimate the importance of self-reflection. I now understand my calling and distinctive mark as a Christian leader in a professional space and the crucibles that attend this divine intentional assignment. I have learned that it is important to examine my assumptions, harness the power of intentional observation, and listen and pay keen attention to what my team forgets to say. I have cultivated and nourished an unwavering faith in God. I have realized that goal setting is highly overrated and accept that we are divinely created to learn from each other.

After spending over thirty years as a Christian instructional leader in a professional space, serving at varying levels and in various capacities throughout the Jamaican education system, I have realized that leadership is not a theory. It is not a place you can travel to or own, not a badge that you can earn, a title you can wear, nor a favorite pastry that you can consume. Leadership is more than just a position or power.

Influential leaders seek meaning and purpose, yearning to make a significant impact on others' lives or contribute to something greater than themselves. Looking back, I owe my progress to the support of divinely appointed destiny helpers, mentors, coaches, wise comforters, and energizing influences.

In the last sixteen years of leadership, some of the most beautiful and fulfilling moments arose from my natural ability to confront challenges, overcome adversity, advocate for positive change, and empower others to surpass their circumstances and achieve transformative outcomes.

Defining Your Leadership Style

One of the most incredible fortunes I was blessed with is playing a role in the growth and development of beginning and, emerging leaders, seasoned executives and middle managers, parents, and students in the education sector.

Ultimately the biggest lessons I have learned as a leader are:

- Leadership is not for everyone. Occupying a leadership position is not the same as leading. We should never mistake spectatorship for leadership.
- Leadership is a transitive verb. It only makes sense if it exerts it action on an object, which can be a team, group, or following. The fact is one hand cannot clap it can only slap.
- Leadership is a calling. When you become a leader, by default, you place your interests at the center of your decisions.
- Leadership is not a selfless role. It is more about who you are than what you do.
- Leadership is not only about what you know. It is also about what you can accomplish with the limited resources you have and how much effort you put into it.
- Leadership must ask questions and listen for the answers. Leaders must question themselves and their motives. They must appreciate questions from others and be open and honest when giving answers.

- Leaders can transition quickly, fail quickly, fix quickly, and die quickly.
- Leaders have to lead themselves to succeed. To go forward in your personal and professional life, you must be intrinsically motivated and courageous enough to take the initial step by yourself.
- Leaders must remain true to their values and beliefs at all times. Commitment, authenticity, consistency, and resilience are essential for being successful.
- Leaders face their fears and believe in themselves, even when no one else does.

The path to success is connecting your true self to your mission.

- Leaders must model followership. They must be willing to step back so others can step forward.
- True leaders grow from their adversity instead of being destroyed by it.
- Christian leaders in a professional space have a distinct, compelling voice. They will experience loneliness, but they are never alone.

Through it all, I have developed my unique leadership style and rhythm and perfected numerous exceptional leadership skills through trial and error. I have learned to trust my instincts. I have mastered the art of finding meaning in adverse events and conquering the most trying circumstances.

I believe every leader must know and establish their signature rhythm. As a leader, you must listen to your organization and team and use the beats to develop your rhythm. Listening is demanding, but crucial for every leader.

However, focused and intentional listening allow you to get in harmony with every beat.

Each beat takes you higher. Each carries an underlined message that points to the unwritten laws of leadership. As an emerging leader, you may experience some difficulty knowing and establishing your rhythm. Unfortunately, at this transactional stage, you have to go at it alone and lead yourself. You have to establish yourself. Overtime, you grow into your leadership style by knowing what makes you tick, ticks you off, what triggers you, and what gives you wings.

The more you learn, listen and interpret, the louder and more pronounced your rhythm becomes. As you become more seasoned, you become strategic. Your leadership inheritance becomes more meaningful, and you begin to adopt a more definitive role based on your context and increasing knowledge and understanding.

Change, adaptability and flexibility become the dynamic force. Each step towards growth and change comes with its own set of challenges. It is a journey of learning, unlearning, relearning, and adaptation.

Each step of this journey demands progressive growth in leadership capacity, mutual accountability, adaptability to complexity, embracing diversity, and creating an organization and culture that enables successful interaction in a complex world.

Each stage leads to the next, and every player must play their part in this suspense drama.

The overarching point is that regardless of whether you are an emerging, developing, seasoned or strategic leader, change and growth takes time.

Effective leadership hinges on how you lead, who you choose to follow, and the pivotal decision to move from mere success to impactful leadership, stepping into the arena of leadership significance.

True and impactful leadership goes beyond merely getting people to follow commands. Lasting and profound leadership transforms into discipleship, empowering individuals to become skilled architects in their fields, capable and confident in their abilities. Empowering others to take charge of their development fosters a culture of expertise and autonomy.

The fact is, any leadership opportunity that is well-executed produces champions and keeps them motivated to succeed. It is not for the complacent. A team is only as strong as its weakest link. Champions are products of complexity. They see the whole and not merely parts. They are capable of holding significant diverse opinions and deeply conflicted positions regarding the 'one size fits all' conventions or customs that we subtly weave into the fabric called leadership.

Indeed, people have diverse preferences and needs, just as different problems require unique solutions. Flexibility and adaptability are essential in addressing the varying circumstances and individuals encountered in life. Leaders given the space and time to understand, appreciate and independently hold the tension of conflicting opposites, usually provide high-order solutions nested in best practices. What we often ignore is that these best practices are not always compatible nor transferable to other settings, and even if we choose to apply them in similar settings, we should be aware of the need to adjust or tailor them if we want to adequately solve our issues.

Trouble Spots

So, what are the things that have proved troublesome on this journey?

That is a good question!

One of the biggest hindrances in this journey is measuring success. This issue is particularly troublesome because of the modern standards that define success based on performance by results instead of the added value or benefits the participants receive on the progressive path of development, growth and proficiency.

We are fascinated with the notion that an effective/transformational leader naturally inspires confidence, loyalty, and hard work. We ignore the reality that others who have just as much vision, skills, and abilities stumble repeatedly. Many leaders find it difficult to understand or accept that change is an exercise in patience and can be a slow-growing fruit because it is not solely dependent on a leader, but also the team.

Additionally, the misconception of equating effective leadership solely with big wins can be misleading. In reality, it is the small achievements, diligently pursued over time, that often pave the way for significant and lasting success. Paying attention to these incremental victories allows for consistent progress and ultimately leads to great outcomes in the end.

Success is written in the fine print. Big things were first small things. When you get lost in the big things that are apparently important, you often forget the little things that truly matter; things that make a difference.

Everyone knows what it means to be in bed with a mosquito or how hard it is to dodge a fly.

Actions and words that go unnoticed in the end are the things that are important because they lead to bigger things. Leaders unknowingly place themselves in danger when they do not pay attention to the little details, as this is the surest way that you are often enlightened to the big things.

'It is numerous small incidents and courtesies of life that make up the sum of life's happiness; and it is the neglect of kindly, encouraging, affectionate words, and the little courtesies of life, which help compose the sum of life's wretchedness'. (White, 2007). Small things matter and can either make or break connections. Small things are the nucleus of effective organizational management, increased revenue, productivity, profitability and outcomes.

It was a light bulb moment for me when I realized that it does not matter what resources we provide. If we do not grasp and use each team member's motivation language, we will never accelerate, change or reshape how the team members view success. I have discovered that motivation looks different for each team member. The key to an organization's success is mobilizing your team members' success through the lens of significance.

Significance in leadership lies in understanding and speaking each team member's motivational language. I will discuss this in upcoming chapters. Until then, I must make the important point that different individuals are motivated by different factors, and effective leaders recognize this diversity. While money may be a powerful motivator for some, others might be driven by praise, authority, or other intrinsic rewards.

Tailoring leadership approaches to address the unique needs and motivations of each team member fosters a more engaged and productive team.

As a Christian leader, another troublesome issue was bridging the gap between secular leadership and Christian leadership.

Bridging the gap between secular and Christian leadership is often portrayed as a simple task—integrating principles from both realms to form a holistic approach. However, the tension between practicality and faith underscores the complexities involved, challenging leaders to navigate this balance with wisdom.

While certain key principles may align between secular and Christian leadership, the values and emphasis of each domain diverge. Strategic thinking, effective communication, and organizational skills are filtered through different interpretations, often lacking the essence of servant leadership, integrity, personal accountability, humility, and compassion that characterize Christian leadership. Recognizing and navigating these disparities is essential in developing a leadership style that reflects the true essence of Christian principles.

As a Christian leader in a professional space, one of my paramount and challenging tasks was discerning my divine appointment, acclimating to my role, grasping the various levels of assignment, and transforming negative situations into new opportunities.

I have discovered that identifying and understanding your God-given assignment is a personal and spiritual journey. Understanding your unique talents and passions and aligning them with a purpose that resonates with your values and beliefs is paramount to your leadership success at any level.

Resilience, the ability to cope and adapt despite loss, stress, and adversity, is a superpower in leadership, particularly in Christian leadership. It goes beyond theory; it comes from personal experience, tested faith and overcoming challenges.

However, resilience is both complex and personal. It is not a fixed trait. Hurley (2022), says, 'we may demonstrate a lot of resilience when it comes to one challenge but struggle more with being resilient when it comes to another stressor' (1).

Conversely, leadership is a life-long journey. It

may not always be clear and straightforward, and it comes with no manual to work through adversity nor turn negative occurrences into new opportunities. One thing I know for sure is that Christian leadership in a professional space, requires careful consideration of various aspects. It requires patience, willpower, persistence, and faith.

My leadership journey has been a long and diverse road, filled with various experiences, challenges, adversities, joys, and successes. Each step has contributed to my growth, making me an overcomer in every sense.

This book portrays my leadership journey, delving into my initial forays into leadership, the invaluable support of those who guided me, he distinctive obstacles I have conquered, and the invaluable lessons I have gained throughout the process.

As a Christian female leader with experience at different levels in a diverse professional space, I initiate a dialogue on purpose-driven leadership, exploring levels of assignment, leading with integrity, cultivating servant leadership, navigating change and adversity, achieving work-life balance, developing discernment and wisdom, and harmonizing faith and work.

I present thought-provoking questions to guide your journey and help you to listen intently to your voice. I encourage you to open your mind, heart, and will, enabling a transformative process that empowers you to emerge as an overcomer.

Whether you are a novice, growing, or experienced

leader, take a moment to reflect on your journey. Reflection is a potent tool that can transform your perspectives, behavior, and outcomes. Ask yourself:

Am I a leader/a Christian leader? What are my defining moments?

Leadership nugget:

"The flip side of your strength is your weakness'

Let us pray:

Dear Lord,

Show me how to view myself as a leader. Grant me your divine discernment to assist me in my defining moments. Amen.

Chapter 2

Heeding the Call to Leadership

'For it is God who is working in you, enabling you both to will and to act for his good purpose' – (Philippians 2:13)

The Routes to Leadership

We become leaders in different ways. People have different experiences and become leaders for various reasons. Whether by opportunity, inheritance, merit, or default – whatever the route one takes, leadership can be challenging.

Self-Appointed Leader

Some leaders are self–appointed or self- declared.

Self-proclaimed leadership occurs when an individual undertakes a leadership role without undergoing any formal selection or receiving approval from those whom they claim to lead.

These leaders are often capable but cannot wait for their turn, or until their change comes. They always undermine the current leader and often disrupt organizations because of their vindictive nature.

They are usually arrogant, self-opinionated, and practice playing the blame game. They often fail to handle authority, power, and promotion. Self-appointed leaders can arise in various contexts, such as informal groups, movements, or organization.

Man Appointed Leader

The audience appoints other leaders. Man-appointed leadership implies that a governing body, an authoritative figure, or group of people elect or chose an individual to lead. The selection process can vary based on the context. It is usually influenced by factors like merit, qualifications, popularity, connections or political considerations, church affiliation, academic ability, experience and intellectual capabilities.

They lead according to man-made standards and rules. These leaders may choose to do what is popular instead of what is right, mainly for approval, induction, and affirmation. They often rely on their connections or qualifications to get by and are more interested in self-gratification rather than the people they swore to serve.

Succession Appointed Leader

Successive appointments aim to ensure flow and a smooth transition of power from one leader to the next. Successive appointment refers to the authority arrangement where an organization or company chooses or appoints individuals to assume roles one after another or in a specific order.

They usually use a hierarchical structure where they select these leaders based on seniority, experience, or a predetermined succession plan.

Shepherd Leader

Timothy Witmer (2017) promotes the shepherd leader model that emphasizes the role of leaders as shepherds. It promotes a leadership approach that prioritizes nurturing, guiding, protecting, and caring for those under their influence. This leadership type is concerned with the psychosocial and emotional intelligence of those they lead. These leaders focus on understanding people, accepting others, being aware of other people's feelings, empathizing, sympathizing, forgiving, and tolerating others. This is mostly used by servant leaders.

God Appointed Leader

God appointment of leadership means that leaders are chosen by a higher power based on a divine calling. These leaders are seen as instruments of a bigger purpose guided by a divine plan. They are strategically placed; they have the responsibilities, resources, and guidance to fulfill their tasks in areas like family, church, workplace, and government.

A God-appointed leader often receives God's favor and changes and adapts based on God's anointing. No human hand can switch, exchange, or supplant this leader without God's consent, nor can they change their position unless they complete their God-given assignment.

With that said, there is obviously a difference between secular leaders and Christian leaders. Both secular leaders and Christian leaders are appointed. Meaning you obtain an office or position and receive the seal and authority to function fully and accomplish a task or a number of assignments. You are the final accountable officer. You are in charge, designated, singled out, and selected to stand out and up and represent. In other words, the buck stops with you. Every leader starts with an appointment, but not every leader is anointed or commissioned.

Christian leaders have a distinctive mark and a divine calling to serve. It does not happen on its own. Your placement is threefold. It is an appointing, anointing, and commissioning.

According to the scripture, when you are under an anointing, it means you get the necessary tools to equip you for carrying out a certain task. God empowers you to accomplish his tasks.

When you are commissioned as a Christian leader, it means you have received a divine assignment and sent out to fulfil a particular purpose. You follow divine instructions. You have a divine mandate.

This shows that you are first chosen or set apart for a task. Then, you are equipped with what you need to succeed, which is the anointing.

Lastly, after these two steps, there is the commissioning. This means you go where God directs you and clearly understand the goals of your assignment, your role, and importance. The commission serves as the measure of your success.

Leadership Success and Leadership Significance

Now that you know about the different types of leadership, you may want to ask yourself these questions;

As a Christian leader, am I a God-appointed or man-appointed leader?

Am I appointed, anointed and commissioned as a leader?

The answer to these questions will prevent you from pouring into a calling that is not yours.

When you identify your assignment and its level, you become a purpose-driven leader.

Simply put, Christian leaders are what I call purposefully commissioned. You can be appointed or anointed, but not commissioned because you are pouring into a calling that does not belong to you.

When you are purposefully commissioned, you are aware of your identity and your belonging. You recognize your worth and confidently present yourself. You are open while also strong. You develop a clear vision, set meaningful objectives, and consistently work towards them. You are confident in your capacity to make important changes and leave a meaningful impact for the long term.

Purposefully commissioned means that your level

of success is dependent or measured by how you handle your leadership assignments and overcome your crucibles.

Significance lies in transforming your challenges into a powerful narrative that becomes a solution, inspiring others to overcome and become champions.

People are empowered, motivated, and inspired because of your credibility, divine authority, where you are, where you have been, what you have learned and how you consistently show up for them.

Undoubtedly, you know that if it had not been for the Lord on your side, you do not know where you would be and how you would survive. You realize you cannot show up as a winner or champion unless you finish the race. This is the difference between a secular leader and a Christian leader.

Secular Leaders vs Christian Leaders

The main difference between Christian and secular leaders lies in the foundation of their guiding principles and the sources of authority they draw upon to make decisions and provide leadership. Christian leaders uphold Christian principles as a lifestyle. Their belief in God, the bible as a moral compass, and the example set by God as a servant leader, govern and guide their decision-making.

Their actions are guided by the pursuit of righteousness based on Christian values. In challenging situations, they demonstrate faith, self-control, wisdom, love, and compassion in every setting.

Secular leaders, on the other hand, tend to center their decision-making and actions on secular ideologies, ethical frameworks, legal systems, societal norms, and considerations of practicality rather than religious doctrines or faith-based principles.

The distinction between Christian leaders and secular leaders is not always absolute or mutually exclusive, as both are accountable to laws, regulations, expectations of the individual, and institutions they represent or serve.

Secular leaders derive their authority from various sources, such as legal frameworks and constitutions, democratic processes, organizational hierarchies, expertise in their field, or the consent and support of the people they lead.

Christian leaders may very well not be accepted from these sources but center their interpretation on the foundation of their faith and their understanding of their role as servants of God and followers of Jesus Christ.

The Distinctive Mark of Christian Leadership.

What makes Christian leadership distinct from secular leadership?

Ted Engstrom notes that the answer can elude us as 'leadership is hard to define, but one characteristic common to all leaders is the ability to make things happen'(1926:25).

Undoubtedly, many secular leaders apply a number of biblical or moral principles in their daily routines, but the difference lies in motives and actions.

Christian leaders do not try to win the favor and approval of men, but of God. Nor do they seek to please everyone. If they try to be popular with men, they would not be a bond-servant of Christ- (Galatians. 1:10).

What is the indispensable mark of Christian leadership?

According to the Cambridge Dictionary, the word 'indispensable' refers to something or someone so good or important that you could not manage without them.

The indispensable mark of Christian leadership is love for God that results in unconditional service to others in the workplace, home, community and country. In His conversation with Peter after His resurrection, God gave Peter a threefold command that clarifies any misconception that we may have about this distinctive mark of Christian leadership.

'Feed my lambs. Feed my sheep, feed my sheep' (John 21: 15 – 17).

This promotes the combined efforts of the Christian leader's motives, actions, and agenda to purposefully influence and transform the lives of others, whilst preparing for this life and the life to come. This is the sign of obedience to God's call to lead.

This indispensable mark of Christian leadership is hinged on living a significant rather than a successful life, referred to as the SOS leadership principle.

John Maxwell (2020) defines success as adding value to yourself and significance as adding value to others. God seals this definition by stating, 'whoever wants to become great among you must be your servant, and whoever wants to be first must be your slave'— even as the Son of Man came not to be served but to serve, and to give his life as a ransom for many. Matt. 20: 26 - 27.

In Christian leadership that follows Christ's model, leadership is about inspiring, assisting, listening, and setting an example for others.

Can a Christian leader be successful without the lens of significance?

We can all agree that there are overwhelming definitions, descriptions, and explanations of successful leadership. However, if you read the literature on successful leadership, you will recognize a distinct pattern.

All include these five top traits of successful leadership/leaders:

- being an excellent communicator
- willingness to delegate and empower
- being committed and passionate.
- being confident
- being honest and full of integrity.

When we dig deeper, we find that this criterion is mainly about embracing worldly notions of successful leadership, that focus on adding value and significance to self. A notion that is strongly denounced by God.

Jesus said, "Do not be conformed to this world, but be transformed by the renewal of your mind, that by testing you may discern what is the will of God, what is good and acceptable and perfect. (Romans.12:2).

It is a challenge for many leaders to break from the traditional mold of leadership and follow new practices. However, we find that whether we are ready or not, willing or not, the paradigm has gradually shifted.

Trinidad Hunt answer, which is extremely relevant to this discussion, is that 'success is winning, and significance is helping others win. Success lives a fingerprint on creation, while significance leaves a footprint on the soul' –D. Trinidad Hunt.

However, Zig Ziglar's (2012) answer put it in perfect context. He says, 'God calls us not to be successful but to be significant. When we focus on significance, success automatically follows.

Christian leaders need to actively stay updated on the changing trends in the technological landscape. They should develop a strategy that enable them to effectively navigate uncertain situations while keeping their focus on making a meaningful impact.

What Is The Winning Strategy Of Leadership For Christian Leaders?

Christian leaders must make nothing or no-one in their life more important that God. In this way, leadership becomes the act of influencing and serving others out of Christ's interests for their lives. This strategy empowers the persons that you lead to identify, understand and usefully accomplish God's purposes through them. (Heb. 10: 24- 25)

They use God's ethical principles as their leadership guide, starting by leading themselves, showing personal responsibility, and setting an example for others.

Relying completely on God to grant them divine insight to understand the current situation, enabling them to confidently take intentional steps that others might perceive as risks. (Prov. 3:5)

This approach helps them steer clear of unnecessary arguments and conflicts (2 Timothy 2:23). They address people with the same respect they would expect if roles were reversed, leading to a foundation of trust and accountability in their leadership.

In addition, they establish robust, amicable, and respectful systems of communication. They speak the truth plainly, use it tactfully, share it completely, and live the truth consistently, (Eph.4:15). They are honorable, steadfast, and thoughtful in their decision-making, thus promoting the greater good of all.

These layers of trust develop a significant and resilient team of champions. Loving God and loving others the way you love yourself is a win- win strategy. Various definitions of leadership have one common thread that sees excellent leadership as the ability to influence the actions and decisions of others. However, this definition is woefully lacking in reference to Christian leadership as it fails to recognize the spiritual dimension of leadership.

The call to be a leader is a great responsibility as "leadership is not a job or a position but a calling," says Maxwell (2008). To be a leader, you must first be a servant for even the Son of man came not to be served but to serve others' (Matt. 20:26). As such, leaders are called to serve. In this context, it requires a special mindset to be a successful leader. I humbly submit that it requires a mind of Christ.

Christian leaders are servants of God, putting Christ's principles first. Their key to effectiveness is having a servant's mindset, prioritizing excellence, integrity, and humility in their leadership. They focus on serving, loving, and growing in faith, relying on God's guidance and strength.

Additionally, as followers of God, Christian leaders are also tasked with serving humanity.

They should embrace a mindset of humility, honest communication, and setting a positive example. Being open to learning from others and embracing growth is essential. Their focus should be on understanding the needs of others to offer inspiration, guidance, and strength.

Lastly, a spiritual growth mindset characterized by faith, prayer, service, integrity, humility, and excellence embodies the belief "I can because God can." Remembering the verse "I can do all things through Christ who strengthens me" (Philippians 4:13) encapsulates a purpose-driven life. It revolves around loving God and your fellow human beings. Serving God naturally leads to loving others. As you contemplate this, ask yourself:

Why was I born? What is my purpose? How can I fulfill my God's given purpose?

Leadership nugget

'If service is below you, leadership is above you – unknown.

Let us pray:

Dear Lord,

Help me identify why I was born and how I can fulfil my God-given purpose. Make me sensitive to the leading of the Holy Spirit as you show me what you want me to do on my path of purpose. Amen.

Chapter 3

Establishing Your Purpose

'Teach me, O Lord, to follow every one of your principles. Give me understanding and I will obey your law. I will put it into practice with all my heart'. (Psalm 119:33-34).

Defining Purpose

The quiet whisper of every human heart is the desperate need for purpose and significance. Leadership, whether secular or Christian, is not a string of coincidences or random circumstances (White, 1844). True leadership is an intentional call to service that derives meaning from an understanding of purpose.

When you do not know your purpose, you are a ragged doll in a masquerade.

No amount of educational qualifications, degrees, or educational courses, erudite scholarly exploits or successes, members in distinguished associations, positions, or influential placements can account for lack of purpose. You cannot find your true purpose wearing a family crest, university crest, and website or feature name.

Just because you are accomplished does not mean you have a sense of purpose. This cannot be acquired solely from affirmations or the applause of men, security of marriage, money or wealth, medals and awards, or even boards and committees.

We often confuse our role with our purpose. Being a sister, doctor, leader, coach, or mentor is your role, but it is not your purpose. You can be clear on your role and still not understand your purpose.

There is a persistent call within each of us to live up to the potential for which we are created.

Purpose gives our lives relevance, determines our priorities, guides our decisions, dictates our partner, and shape our choices. Your purpose in this world is higher and more important than your role in the world. Living your moments of destiny is the reason why you were created.

Understanding Purpose

There are many leaders in the world, and yet purpose-driven leadership is scarce. This is so because leading with purpose and on purpose is not petty.

It requires you to recognize that we all have a mission or assignment that is bigger than we are.

It is not a popularity contest, or stage show overly concerned with self-gratification. Rather, it is an understanding of your life mission that comes from an inner drive and a sacred place of empowerment. It constantly reminds us that our current or past circumstances do not limit us. Instead, it is up to us to act and make the most of our God-given potential, authority, and influence. To take the right actions, you must ask yourself: *Why was I born?*

Before we were born, God gave each of either us a purpose, calling, and assignment that we can discover or completely miss. In Jeremiah 1:5, God explains that before He formed you in the womb, he knew you, set you apart, and appointed you. This means that he purposed you to be born in the generation that you are.

You are in the right era. It was not an accident. You are in the right place at the right time. 'Thou art come to the kingdom for such a time as this.' (Esther 4:14).

It is possible to have an intrinsic yearning or restlessness that there is something you must do or should be doing, but it remains oblivious to you. This can be troublesome because you cannot use what you do not know you have.

On the other hand, if, like Jonah, we resist, God will ultimately get the glory.

Once God has set your life's purpose, it remains unchangeable. No human effort can close doors He opens or open doors He closes. God is the ultimate architect of purpose, uniquely tailored for each individual. His intentions for you are exclusively yours and cannot be emphasized enough.

Your purpose is the reason for which you are created or exist. Although God has a purpose for everyone, and works through us to fulfill His purpose, he does not force us to comply. God's purpose is good, but we are not. God desires your voluntary, conscious, intentional, and purposeful involvement.

Purpose is a collaboration between the human and the divine. A contract, if you will. This contract obligates us to identify, possess and claim our why.

When you know your why, you activate your purpose and God's divine favor. You possess the divine authority, and influence. You possess the divine power. The inevitable result is godly self-fulfillment and contentment. This is the ultimate gain.

Misinterpreting the "why" can derail your purpose. True leadership necessitates questioning "why." Ministry thrives when "why" takes precedence over "what." Constantly fixating on personal struggles, external actions, deficiencies, and feelings lulls your purpose into dormancy. Fear becomes a self-imposed confinement, confining you to a lesser leadership role.

You cannot change or improve things if you do not ask why. When you ask meaningful questions, such as, why am I going through this? *Why am I a leader? Why was I placed here, of all places? Why should I do this?* The answers can revolutionize your entire life, leadership, and ministry. Your leadership takes on meaning and results in significance. It carries influence and you are able to rightly divide your talents and skills.

Every practicing leader, Christian or secular, will confirm that the path of leadership is not easy, and sometimes we buckle under pressure. This can make us question God's purpose or resist our purpose. During the darkest times on my leadership journey, I received employment opportunities that were truly enticing and appeared greener, lush, and more fruitful. As I prayerfully scrutinized the finer details, I knew they did not fit God's purpose for my life.

There are other times when skillful hypocrites wore themselves out ensuring that a situation went badly for me, but God worked everything out for my good. We often have to be patient as we press into our purpose. Hasty decisions and the things we value can have serious ramifications and take us out of alignment.

Christian leaders in a professional space must always remember that God exalts nothing above His purpose. No purpose of God can be thwarted (Job 42:2).

God's purpose is the one that lasts. To accomplish his purpose, he will use adversity, confrontation, conflict, disappointments, delays and pain. Purpose-driven leaders are immune to complacency. God sends challenges, like a Penna, to stir and refocus you on your purpose. To truly make an impact, you must comprehend your God-given identity. The pivotal inquiry is: *What is my purpose?* Finding this answer is the essential stride toward recognizing and comprehending your purpose.

How Can I Identify My Purpose?

Each of us have the ability to identify the overarching purpose of our lives and live from that knowledge. Understanding your life purpose helps you to start leveraging it powerfully.

Identifying your purpose gives your life meaning, a sense of control, satisfaction, and ultimately significance.

It's the specific way in which you engage with life that makes use of all that you are and draws on your unique experiences, talents, abilities, and interests in a way that helps you achieve your highest goals while being a servant of God and of service to others.' Kathy Carpino (2018).

Carpino (2018) says 'the key to uncovering your purpose is to start behaving as if you're worthy enough to have one by honoring the things that you love to do'. One helpful habit is helping others. By offering your skills, talents, and abilities to aid others, your purpose starts to crystallize. This act initiates a journey of self- discovery, unveiling your genuine passions.

Delve into activities and topics you enjoy and resonate with, those that hold meaning in your life.

Identifying those, you consistently assist, the recurring ways you offer help, your natural inclinations to support others and your aspirations for new forms of assistance can provide valuable insights for understanding your purpose.

Some of us are capable of doing different things. The way individuals respond to the things we do, and the unified theme of the responses can aid you in identifying and understanding your passions. Valuing constructive criticism and objective feedback can fuel your purpose.

Cultivating self-awareness is another method to uncover and learn about your purpose. Reflect on what motivates you, what fuels your energy, what you are ready to devote yourself to, who benefits from your assistance, and the ways you genuinely offer help. Remember that your tasks and responsibilities can evolve over time.

Finding your purpose does not mean you change what you currently do. It simply means that you add meaning to your life and give your actions and assignments significance. When you are clear about your purpose, it is easier at each level of the assignment to answer the question, *'How can I fulfill my purpose?*

Purpose vs Assignment

Kathryn H. Creasy notes that 'our purpose is why we are on earth; whilst our calling is the path, we take to fulfill our purpose. The assignments are the tasks we do along the way. I highlighted that God created you and every person for a specific assignment on this earth and that our existence is not a mistake.

Before God created you, He decided what role He wanted you to play on earth. He planned exactly how

He wanted you to serve Him, and then He created and shaped you for that task. You are the way you are because you were made specifically for a specific assignment on earth. https://pastors.com/god-shaped-you-to-serve- him

Esther was set aside before her birth to become a beauty queen in God's divine plan and along with Mordecai persuade the king to cancel an order for the termination of the Jews (Esther 4:14).

Mary was set aside before her birth to perfectly conceive and along with Joseph to secure the entry of Jesus into the human world (Luke 1:30).

Deborah's was set aside before she was born to be the only female judge in Israel's history to secure forty (40) years of peace for the Israelites. (Judges 5: 7 -12).

Moses was set aside before he was born for his parents' enemy to raise him and to tend sheep in order to fulfill his assignment to bring the children of Israel from Egypt (Exodus. 3:10).

Joshua' was set aside before he was born to come after Moses, to lead the children of Israel across river Jordan to the Promised Land (Joshua 1:1-2).

David was set aside before he was born to kill Goliath and later become the king of Israel (Exodus 3:10).

Dorcas was set aside before she was born to help clothe the poor in her community. (Acts 9:36).

Jonah was set aside before he was born to carry the repentance message to Nineveh so that they could repent and avert the disaster that God was to bring upon Nineveh (Jonah 1:1-2).

John the Baptist was set aside before he was born to prepare the way for Jesus (Luke 3; 16).

When each had completed their assignments and fulfilled their purpose, God laid them to rest.

It may take us a minute or forty years to understand our purpose. No matter how long it takes, we will not leave this earth until we complete the assignment that God created and destined us to do.

Our life holds little meaning or significance if we cannot answer these questions:

What is my highest and best self?

Did I make the best use of what God gave me?

Did I fulfill the tasks that bound me to my calling and purpose?

When you identify and understand your specific assignment, the levels of assignments, and you finish it, you triumphantly embrace your destiny.

Levels of Assignment

I believe that five fundamental levels relate to God's assignments: Preparation or Feeding, Rations, Anointed, Appointed, and Commissioned

At the preparation and feeding level, you undergo training and preparation. The problem you must solve is big enough to see, but small enough to deal with. At this level, you ask, seek, and knock.

Asking means that you pray to God and ask him to reveal to you your assignment/s. At this level, your assignments are usually straightforward, with the added benefit that you are active, energetic, and enthusiastic. Simple assignments are easier to attempt and obey.

'If you fully obey the Lord your God and carefully follow all his commands I give you today, the Lord your God will set you high above all the nations on earth. Deuteronomy 28:1

In my earlier experience as a Christian leader, I discovered that my overarching purpose centered on advocacy, support, and empowerment. Every assignment required me to advocate, support, or empower people by changing mindsets, outcomes, and lives.

Thus, I empowered the individuals in my white-collar community with certification programs, work programs, Healthy Relationships seminars and exchange programs.

I also advocated for the change of policies, standards, and procedures that were no longer fulfilling their intended use or securing the desired outcomes. I supported community and staff members during adversity and loss. I sadly remember when my organization lost three students in the span of two months. That wasn't all. Several staff members, including myself, experienced a huge loss. We went through a wilderness season that included the loss of numerous family members in a short time.

In one instance, one staff member lost three family members in a month; two tragically, and the other succumbed after a long period of illness.

However, my specific assignment as a Christian leader in this space was community building. I was purposefully commissioned to change the fixed mindset of all stakeholders to a growth mindset. That became the most challenging assignment I have ever been given.

I remember praying to God. My prayer sounded something like this:

Dear Lord,

I do not know why you chose me. Show me how you have equipped me for your Kingdom's work and lead me to the people and places where you are calling me to carry out my tasks. In Jesus name. Amen.

The first assignment allowed me to find my bearings. That is how God works. When he stamps your purpose on you, He equips you and prepares the needed provisions. However, you do not get the provision until you step into your vision, and you do not get the resources until you connect your sources. I used the connections God gave me beforehand to provide the financial resources to:

- Enhance the physical appearance of the institution by repairing the doors and windows that were over fifty years old
- Enhance the corridors
- Supply well-needed technological equipment and software such as computers and monitors
- Create a safe and secure learning environment by enclosing the institution and installing security cameras
- Upgrade the feeding program and facilities by providing state of the art kitchen equipment and beautifying the environment.
- Conduct Parental Workshops and Healthy relationship seminars
- Provide fully funded recreational retreats for all employees.

I was the idealistic optimist. Everything was peachy. My confidence vibrations were at a high frequency.

"Seeking" involves praying for God's perspective on your mission and the way you will be prepared for it. "Knocking" means persistently praying until you gain a clear understanding.

When you are at the sustenance level, you move from obedience to a more courageous place.

Your assignments begin to get more challenging, but you are no longer afraid. You are now a realistic enthusiast. You possess creativity, compassion, and courage. You know that all things are working for your good, and you are beginning to understand the intentionality of God.

At this level, God uses each challenge to train you to listen and open yourself, i.e., your mind, head, and heart. Now He is able to guide and groom you at every opportunity to fulfill your assignment. Most importantly, you are not easily daunted because you are beginning to accept that you have been raised for this very purpose, 'that I might show you my power and that my name might be proclaimed in all the earth" (Exodus 9:16).

At the anointed level, your assignments get more formidable. You enter a wilderness season of preparation that God keeps you uninformed about. You are tested, tried, and ready to give up your assignment. You are sorely tempted to become an informed pessimist. Your joy days greatly diminish as your joy killers and naysayers increase.

This level troubles your soul. At this level, everything that can be shaken is shaken. Your faith, skills, talents and abilities, your friendships, relationships, influence, value and worth. Every voice of accusation and every enemy to success is present and forcefully active at this level.

This includes the voice of judgement, cynicism, fear, blame, and defeat. During this period, you must never lose sight that you are not alone.

All past and present God-appointed, purpose-driven Christian leaders have reached this stage.

David wasn't the initial choice among his brothers, rather he was picked when no other option seemed viable. Ridiculed by his brothers and mocked by Goliath, he had to hold onto his purpose amidst challenges. Similarly, Esther and Mordecai faced plotting from Haman, leading to a collective fast and eventual triumph of God's purpose. Moses reached this point with lasting consequences, unable to enter the Promised Land. Mary and Joseph encountered doubt, isolation, and disgrace, yet their divine assignment prevailed.

I got more than my fair share at this level. When it came to fulfill my assignments, which included changing mindsets, informal structures, setting boundaries, and establishing organizational cultures and norms, things became quite intense. I endured accusations, verbal abuse, confrontations, conflicts, leadership loneliness, isolation, and faced ethical dilemmas, betrayals and loss.

These gifts were bestowed upon me by significant figures: parents, well-meaning yet misguided advisors, and those who pretended to be helpful but were insincere.

Such experiences can certainly knock you off your feet or take you off guard, but because you are surprised does not mean that you are not prepared.

I can recall being juxtaposed between the expectations of the church groups aligned with my organization, and the political influences aligned to my institution. I was under pressure from both groups because I refused to allow my title to become a ball and chain that prevented me from being who I am or caused me to relinquish my mantra that I would stand for the truth, through the heavens fall.

Taking a determined path to make right choices rather than popular ones led to my unpopularity. An incident at one of my organization's school leaving exercise further exemplified this when the leader, due to personal reasons, and misinformation orchestrated opposition against me after a vote of thanks misstep. This was distressing for several reasons: it involved a Christian leader acting un-Christian, who harbored resentment for a year while appearing friendly, and whose unjust behavior could have affected innocent students from his congregation, if I did not have moral courage as a leader to vigorously oppose it.

I encountered a situation where two married couples joined my staff, with both male's spouse at senior management levels. Negligence was apparent in various instances and the necessary memos, reprimands, reminders, or warnings were not given.

Additionally, family and community loyalty created complexities. A substantial portion of my employees had deep community ties, attended the institution, and returned as employees, which was negatively affecting the institution.

Their personal and community connections hindered objective consensus and support. Proximity exacerbated personal issues affecting professional decisions.

Often, significant choices were influenced by emotions outside of formal meetings. Shifting this paradigm was an immense challenge.

During an election campaign, two employees displayed unprofessional behavior towards clients who did not align with a specific political stance. When they were professionally addressed regarding their misconduct and asked to respond to the clients' grievances, the employees responded with rebellion. This was because of their connections with the hierarchy with a similar political persuasion.

Then to add fire to the fury, when the matter was referred to the Personnel committee. The employees did not receive a reprimand or a warning because they were active members of the community, the church, and was affirmed as political activists who were only displaying their loyalty to the right political base.

In that climate, an undesirable tension developed within the PTA, the school, and an unwanted discord was distributed among staff members related to the offended and the offender. This called for strategic decision- making, conflict resolution strategies, and ultimatums.

Further tensions emerged from the contrast between the technocrats' bottom-up approach and the disconnect between theory and practice, evident in the emphasis on data-driven rather than solution- oriented strategies.

Misunderstandings, controversy, and toxicity punctuate any exchange in which you request quality support, stakeholder accountability, mutual understanding, and respect rather than platitudes and promises.

Despite this, God's purpose always prevailed. You eventually realize that those who God has provided for you are more than those who are against you. Furthermore, at every level of assignment, God remains with us. Not only does He give His angels charge over thee, to keep thee in all thy ways (Psalm 34:7), but the faithful are under the constant care of angels (Hebrews 1:14), who guide them and direct them perpetually.

Failing to fulfill your tasks at this stage results in a prolonged period and missed opportunities. It hinders your purpose's realization. While you cannot skip seasons, adeptly handling them is crucial for progressing to your destined level.

When you get to the appointed level, your assignments appear almost impossible.

However, because you have managed your seasons in your anointing, you now rely on hopeful realism. You walk by faith and not by sight. You realize that all things are possible with Christ and that with your experiences, you acquired wisdom. You now move systematically undeterred into the fulfillment of your purpose. Your current vantage point shapes your perspective, which then guides your actions.

You learn that the whole is greater than the sum of the parts. You now understand that you are purposefully commissioned. At this level, you take everything in stride. You allow nothing to disturb your peace of mind or distract you from your purpose. Confrontation, conflict, loss, grief, betrayal, disappointment, criticism, accusation, alienation, shame nor reproach. You pass all the tests. You endure. You conquer. You overcome. You are resilient.

This is because you have acquired a 'warriors' mindset. This mentality is because you now know who God is, what he can do and how he has kept you. You now know how to choose your battles wisely and you stop making excuses. You no longer engage in the blame game. You revel in tough situations and recover from setbacks because you have learned to rely on God's presence, power, providence and performance.

How does a good mental health help leader to cultivate resilience and leadership significance? Leaders are required to inspire and lead their team and make tough decisions whilst dealing with high levels of stress and pressure. Thus, leaders and Christian leaders especially must 'keep their mental health, healthy' (Testimonio, 2023). When we focus on honoring God in this way, it shows that we completely rely on and trust God to direct our steps and chart our leadership path and are not leaning into our own understanding, deceiving and relying totally on self. It shows that we are leading with self- care and purpose. I have expanded the issue of self-care and purpose in another chapter.

Suffice it to say, we should not ignore the critical role of mental health in peaking a leader's confidence vibrations, cultivating resilience and maximizing significance. Leaders with good mental health are more likely to regulate their emotions and remain calm and composed under pressure. Their resilience level is usually very high, and they can cope with stress, disappointment and /or failure more effectively. This helps them to persevere through difficult times and lead their team with confidence. This fosters trust and better working relationships.

They are able to connect and relate to their team members needs and communicate with greater sensitivity. They are more equipped to make rational, informed decisions and solve complex problems and consider various options.

Leaders who pay attention to or prioritize their mental wellbeing are better equipped to navigate the complexities of leadership, make crucial and sound decisions and positively influence their team and organizations. This helps to foster a more productive, profitable and positive work and leadership culture.

When your confidence level is at its highest frequency, you become the leader you would want to follow. Your inner voice does not change no matter how difficult challenges or things get. Your mind is at the stage where anything you desire is possible. You are now a leadership disciple. You are at perfect peace. You understand your assignments. You walk in your assignments and fulfil your purpose.

Assignments Help Us to Fulfill our Purpose

An assignment is the task that God gives each of us to start us on the path of our destiny. The important thing is we sometimes do not understand our assignment. However, God is not in the business of giving you an assignment and expecting you to fail. He equips you as you go about performing and growing in an understanding of your purpose. "For I know the plans I have for you, declares the Lord, plans for welfare and not for evil, to give you a future and a hope." (Jeremiah 29:11)

Once you identify your God-given or spiritual assignment and understand your earthly assignments, you collaborate with Him and involve Him systematically, as you allow Him to lead you into His divine purpose for your life.

How does an understanding of each level propel me towards fulfilling my purpose? The answer is simple. When you understand your assignments, you know the timings in your life, the seasons, and the actions that you must take at each level.

You do not water when you should be planting, you do not sow when you should be reaping, and you do not walk when you should be running. You step into your timing.

Can I jump or miss a level? Mastering each level is important as it prepares you for the next.

Wherever there is preparation, there is pruning. At each level, you are being pruned to produce. You cannot walk before you creep. You cannot be sustained before being prepared. You cannot struggle with identifying and understanding your purpose or assignment and accomplish it. When you struggle, you become disengaged or distracted. Your actions become premature and do not bear fruit.

What do I need to do to master each level?

Listen to the desire in your heart. God placed it in your heart for you to do and accomplish it.

Know the why. There is a different 'why' at each level. Pause every time you have a cause and ask for God's perspective. God helps you with every assignment that you have, that he gives you if you are open for that to happen. Pray for clarity and understanding at each level. Constantly reflect. At each level, ask yourself the question:

Whose work am I doing?

Understanding Jurisdiction – Standing in Your Assignment

When God appoints you, He gives you power and authority to fulfill your purpose through your assignments. Whatever God calls you to do; he equips you with the knowledge, the right people, and the right resources at the right time.

God has designed a balance of authority and power in four jurisdictions or authority points; the home, church, professional space, and government 'to serve others and to marshal them toward a goal ordained by God' – (Drucker, 2021). This indicates the necessity to enhance your understanding of your authority and capability, empowering you to embrace the responsibilities of Christian leadership, regardless of its context.

Authority is essentially the divine empowerment bestowed upon you through your gifts and your role in various domains. This facilitates the acquisition of experience, expansion of your influence, and broadening of your service to both God and humanity.

You need to understand that with this authority comes personal accountability. You are your greatest asset; your authority is within you. You have unique gifts, talents, and abilities that only belong to you. You are fearfully and wonderfully made. That is your DNA of authority, your inner identity, and your call to always go higher. You have great value, and a divine price tag. God does not have a half-price sale or a wholesale discount card on you. You decide if you want to be a vessel of honor or dishonor.

Some people believe that authority is about power. For me, authority is not so much about power, but more about permitting yourself to become or to be the person God created you to be.

Knowing that you already have the authority from your Creator, you have to accept that authority and walk in it.

Divine power originates from God as you grasp and embrace your authority. While someone in authority typically holds power, a Christian leader's power is demonstrated through their positive impact on others. When your actions empower, inspire, guide, or fortify others, you are effectively exercising your authority.

Aligning Your Assignments with Your Personal Values

You raise your impact level, influence, and power, when you align your assignments, values, and beliefs with your purpose. Each of us has our own calling to answer, and our passion to embrace. Your values point to who you are at your core emotionally, behaviorally, cognitively, and spiritually. Our values do not lean towards us; we lean towards what we value.

Your values influence your actions, relationships, and overall life. It guides you as you make big decisions and influences what you want to achieve professionally and personally.

We sometimes alter or change our values overtime as we grow and mature, or as our circumstances and situations change our perspectives.

Nonetheless, without personal values, we will not know what we want to achieve or what we are capable of achieving. Committing to uncovering what we value in life will always work in our favor. Our values help us to prioritize what is important in our lives and give us a better understanding of ourselves.

Lacking clear values makes tasks harder, blurs focus, and leads to doubt in our choices and decisions. Our values protect and nurture our joy and peace to our point of reference. It makes us more passionate about our life purpose and motivates us to do well.

When we build relationships with our values, we screen our influences and use them to combat feelings of insecurity and inferiority. We practice what we preach. We embody authenticity, honesty, integrity, and truth. We set goals that work towards our purpose rather than against it.

When we struggle to find ways to improve our authority, power, impact, influence, and coexistance with a greater sense of purpose, it is because we have not identified and defined our core values.

It is necessary that our assignments, our values, and beliefs, be in symphony with each other so that our intentions and actions can lead us towards fulfilling our purpose, protect, and nurture us at the same time.

A clear sense of our values, merged with a strong sense of purpose, make it easier to tap into your assignments and remain focused and committed. When you make decisions aligned with your personal values, you will feel like your truest self.

As you reflect, ask yourself these questions:

What is important to me? How do I feel when I go against my values? How do I align my assignment with my purpose?

Leadership Nugget:

'If your path is difficult, it is because your purpose is bigger than you thought'.

- Unknown

Let us pray:

Dear Lord,

You have created me for good works. Help me to identify and complete my assignments to the best of my ability. Guide my steps and help me to trust you, knowing that you are with me and that my worth comes from whom I am in you.

Amen.

Chapter 4

Understanding Christian Leadership

"Many are the plans in a person's heart, but it is the Lord's purpose that prevails" (Proverbs 19:21) for it is God who works in you to will and to act in order to fulfill his good purpose" (Philippians 2:13).

Have you ever got what you wanted and then didn't want what you got? Landing the leadership position that you want can be thrilling. After all, it is a reward for your academic preparation, hard work, and perseverance.

However, you will find that you are spending majority of your time dealing with the human side of leadership. This involves finding yourself supervising a set of employees, who all offer and need something different.

Additionally, you may have inherited interpersonal conflicts, disengaged, disgruntled, and disillusioned followers, differing emotions, loyalties, and complex personalities.

Consequently, you have a hard time prioritizing what you need to accomplish, and very soon, your career becomes your life.

I have learned as a leader that you should never confuse your career with your life. You cannot tell when your organization will stop loving you, and the position does not make the man; it is the integrity of character-Thoreau (2020). "What you get by achieving your goals is not as important as what you become by achieving your goals." – Henry David (2020).

At the end of your career, you must be able to love yourself and live comfortably.

Ellen White says, 'the higher the position a man occupies, the greater the responsibility that one has to bear, the wider will be the influence that he exerts and greater the need of dependence on God. Ever should he remember that with the call to work comes the call to walk circumspectly before his fellowman'.

Christian leaders in their professional space must be people of strong purpose, who are not easily moved, can lay down every selfish interest, and give their all. They are wise leaders whose actions match their words. They are great role models who show integrity. Integrity is who you are and how you act. How you act, is who you are -Nathaniel Branden (2019).

Modus Operandi of Christian Leaders

After more than twenty-five years as a Christian leader, I have learned that effective Christian rule needs to embrace and integrate these six models of leadership to articulate an authentic, vibrant, and dynamic action plan; moral leadership, responsive leadership, strategic leadership, situational leadership, small things leadership and servant leadership. These models serve to empower team members to become responsible and genuine leaders i.e., gaining significance in their organization, church, neighborhood and community.

They have a strong sense of who they are (leading with purpose and on purpose) and are open-minded (possess a growth mindset).

Moral Leadership

Christian leaders lead themselves and others, guided by ethical principles and values that have a reference point in godliness. They 'do not withhold any good from those to whom it is due, when it is in the power of their hands to do so' – (Proverbs 3:27) Emphasis added.

Leaders who practice moral leadership prioritize doing what is right, demonstrate integrity and consider the long-term consequences of their actions on those they lead and the society in which they operate.

Noah is a prime example of moral leadership. He took responsibility for himself and focused on what God had called him to do. Although the work was hard, and people surely judged, mocked, and ridiculed him, he faithfully followed God. He chose to do what was right over what was easy or popular.

God calls Christian leaders to a very high calling when he appoints them in a professional space. He expects them to be resilient, honest, and fair, and set a positive example in their personal and public life.

By virtue of this positive display of character, they are able to hold all of their employees to the same ethical standards. In this way, they promote a sense of equity and inclusion in the workplace.

One of the most important components of moral leadership is emotional intelligence. This requires us to not only understand and manage our own emotions, but also points to how we read, recognize, and influence the emotions of others.

As a Christian leader, my values resonate with moral leadership. However, moral leadership can be very troublesome. It is not for the faint- hearted. This model can sometimes give you feelings of loneliness and isolation as you endeavor to be fair in all your undertakings and avoid corrupt practices as earnestly as avoiding contracting the COVID virus.

I have had to maintain a high degree of emotional intelligence and be a positive thinker as I tried to avoid office politics. Most importantly, I worked to comprehend how my personal principles align with my organization, and I upheld them while making tough yet significant choices.

There were painful and reaffirming moments involved with always taking responsibility for the consequences of my actions, both good and bad, and cooperative responsibility for the actions of my team.

In the tough moments, I had to display courage. There were also instances when dealing with challenging workplace situations that I was accused of being unfair in my decision-making; despite the fact that I avoided being bias, neither practice favoritism, and only promoted transparency, communicate standards, and established organizational values and lovingly reminded team members of the ethical code of conduct.

There were also times when I had to take a stand against ethical violations while promoting a culture of unity and inclusion.

Responsive Leadership

This required me to be highly responsive and attuned to the needs and personality types of my team members. Although I am one person, I was required to be all things to all persons.

Christian leaders in their role as servants of God and their assignments, have to acquire the ability to adapt to and respond effectively to changing circumstances and the needs of team members and stakeholders. They must be attentive to feedback, open to new ideas, and highly flexible in their decision-making. They must learn to prioritize effective communication, collaboration, and inclusiveness to ensure that their leadership style aligns with the evolving needs and expectations of those they lead.

The story of Ruth is a perfect example of responsive leadership. Although Naomi had lost her sons, she accepted that Ruth and Orpah were still young and deserved to live happy lives. With this in mind, she encouraged them to leave her and remarry. Orpah chose to leave and Ruth choose to remain. Ruth recognized that leaving Naomi would result in a life of need and scarcity. Her reaction to the unfortunate turn of events was to prioritize her mother-in-law's well-being and strive diligently to provide for her. She exhibited responsive leadership by considering the broader perspective and finding ways to serve others before herself. This demonstrates a test and a virtue of Christian leadership.

Education Elements (2019) describes responsive leadership as an approach that 'creates the culture, structures and systems for organizational learning, so that the people who make up the organization are able to learn from and with each other, developing their own skills and expertise'. Senge (2018)

Peter Senge, views responsive leadership as an approach that 'encourages employees to think outside the box and work with other employees to find the best answer to any problem' via five disciplines; personal mastery, mental models, shared vision, team learning, and systems thinking.

In my experience, responsive leadership is a crucial model for Christian leaders in the workplace.

This approach fosters personal growth through self-responsibility and collaborative involvement. Each team member, including the leader, must cultivate self-discipline to consistently refine their individual vision, channel their efforts, cultivate patience, and confront reality transparently and truthfully. In a result-oriented instead of a value-added context, this can be hard. Christian leaders must demonstrate the ability to compare new ideas with internal images of how the organization, stakeholders, and the community work. The mental models and expectations must coincide to provide direction, so they do not limit innovation and creativity.

Team members at all levels must have a shared vision and hold a common picture of the desired outcome and future that the organization seeks to create. The leader must develop ways to guide, coach, and mentor team players to align and develop their capacities, creating the results that they truly desire.

Every team player must recognize and understand that the organization consists of interconnected parts. They must understand their role and the long-term detrimental effects of any misalignment.

Strategic Leadership

This possibility of misalignment in leadership is a real issue. For this reason, strategic leadership is a relevant integration for Christian leaders. It involves setting a clear vision and direction for your organization or team, formulating, and using the right strategies to achieve short and long-term goals.

Christian leaders are 'servants' with a growth mindset. When you identify your purpose and understand your God-given assignments, you always formulate a plan because you do not lack wisdom nor faith. It comes from God. Your faith comes from God's promise. 'I know the plans I have for you, plans to prosper you' (Jeremiah 29:11) that is to connect your resources to your God-given sources and the proper provisions to your vision. This is to give you hope and a future', which is the expected end.

Thus, Christian leaders who integrate this model

in the workplace are forward-thinking and have a big-picture perspective. They analyze the internal and external environment, identify opportunities and risks, and make decisions that align with the overall strategic objectives of their organization.

David was such a leader. He did not defeat Goliath with might in combat or physical armor. His armor was a foolproof God–given strategy, in which he used a slingshot and a stone to strike Goliath in his forehead and defeat him. We can also remember that as a strategic thinker, David constantly used strategy in battle. His selected soldiers were the men of Issachar – (1 Chron.12:32), who he handpicked for the simple reason that they could think and plan strategically.

Strategic leadership mobilizes and inspires others to work towards a shared goal.

An effective leader who is forward-thinking, who is able to mobilize and inspire others to work towards a shared good, is situational.

Situational Leadership

Situational leadership is an adaptive leadership model that emphasizes matching the leadership approach to the specific needs and capabilities of individuals or teams in different situations.

First, situational leaders assess the competence and commitment of their team members and adjust their leadership style accordingly. Moses practiced situational leadership when God instructed him to prepare Joshua to take up leadership (Exodus 17:14), what we refer to in the professional space as succession planning. Why? There were character and skill development gaps. Joshua was not yet ready.

Moses identified the areas that Joshua needed to improve and master and matched his leadership actions to his needs.

Second, they may provide guidance and direction to those who are inexperienced or uncertain, offer support and encouragement to those who are capable but lack confidence, and dedicate authority to those that are highly skilled and motivated. Jesus perfectly exemplified this type of leadership in his quest to successfully prepare his disciples to succeed him. He instructed them when they were uninformed (Sermon on the Mount), directed them when they were confused (feeding of the five thousand), prodded them when they were reluctant (The Miraculous Catch of Fish at the Lake of Galilee), and encouraged them when they were downhearted (Jesus' Ascension to heaven).

Throughout His ministry, He gave his disciples assignments, worked with them, guided them, interacted with them, responded according to their needs, and empowered them. Most importantly, he did not ignore the small things. He used them as guides. When they were ready, he commissioned them.

Small Things Leadership

Despite the rigors of his ministry of healing, raising from the dead, preaching, admonishing, and 'discipling', Jesus intentionally focused on the importance of paying attention to the small details and actions that contribute to the overall significance of outcomes. He emphasized the importance of small things. 'One who is faithful in a very little is also faithful in much, and one who is dishonest in a very little is also dishonest in much. – (Luke 16:10). Small things leadership whilst prioritizing acts of kindness, appreciation, and attention to detail and creating a positive work environment and fostering strong relationships with their team members, understand that, it is the 'little foxes that spoil the vineyard' – (Songs of Solomon 2:15). 'Simply put the small things that seem to be nothing can destroy the big things.

I learned some distance into my leadership journey to pay attention to small things: a change in expression, silence, a sigh, and an unprovoked statement, the absence of a key team player in crucial decision-making and/or a sudden familiarity or overwhelming support from a highly disgruntled team player when no one moves to defend you or help you. I grew in the understanding that even seemingly insignificant gestures, decisions, or behaviors can significantly affect morale, motivation, and productivity.

I comprehend that team members and the leader can view the same data, share the same experiences, and yet hold entirely distinct perspectives. I developed the art of paying attention to the people I am speaking with, so I can observe their body language and facial expression and listen to their tone to see how I am triggering them or if they are shutting down. I often asked myself some soul-searching questions on the lonesome road of leadership, *'What would I want someone to say to me if I was in that position? How can I bring them back to the real issue?'*

I can assure you, emotional intelligence is grossly underrated in these small 'crushing' leadership moments, and stress can certainly erode self-control. Small things leadership can help leaders to set the right boundaries.

Leadership levels can cross.

At this juncture or crossing, team players can step out of their roles into another person's role, especially in a crisis when you need all hands-on deck.

This small act can be improperly interpreted. Excessive appreciation can later become a big battle as persons begin to appoint their post. This seemingly small yet necessary thing can reduce a leader to goal and bargaining points of their subordinates or produce disengaged, disgruntled, or disillusioned team members.

Nonetheless, Jesus was prepared to serve everyone, even those who would eventually betray him, by sacrificing himself and with great love. That is the heart of servant leadership.

Servant Leadership

Servant leadership does not diminish your position, influence, or significance as a Christian leader. It actually enhances it. Christian leaders seek ways they can add value to others, and the primary way they can do so is by serving them.

Your acts of service demonstrate humility and love for your followers or team players. By lifting others, you lift yourself and give authenticity, meaning and purpose to your life, intentions, and actions. Servant leadership is not a new concept. In fact, it is the model of leadership that unites all other models previously mentioned. It is the fulcrum of Christian leadership, especially in a professional space. It embodies the theme of significance that God advocates for Christian leaders at every level.

It is easy to become addicted to the power and authority attached to be a leader. Jesus highlighted this when he commissioned his disciples. He emphasized that their practice of leadership was to be distinctively different from the current model of leadership practiced by the Pharisees and the self-serving, self-seeking, and domineering style of leadership, often found in the world. 'Whoever wants to be a leader among you must be your servant and whoever wants to be first must be your slave- Matt. 20: 26 – 27.

He was the perfect example of servant leadership as he ministered to all and sundry and eventually gave his life as a ransom – Matt. 19:10.

Servant leaders need the humility to accept assistance from others, acknowledging that anyone can be a vessel of help. They should also be open to learning and listening to those under their guidance, acknowledging the possibility of better ideas or alternative valuable viewpoints.

Servant leadership is the opposite of lording or exercising authority over others. Instead, it is about being a servant to others and following the example of Jesus. Rather than focusing solely on their own power and authority, servant leaders actively seek to support and empower their team members, enabling them to reach their full potential. Conversely, servant leadership is motivated by love, not by selfish ambition or pride. It is based on the security of knowing one's identity and position in God, not on seeking recognition or approval from others. It is willing to initiate service to others, even to those who are undeserving or ungrateful (John 13:1- 5). It is not about imposing one's own will or agenda, but about following God's will and serving his purposes (John 13:12-17; Romans 1:1).

The Purpose Driven Leader

The powerful symmetrical alignment of these models is the sum total of authentic leadership. Authentic leadership is

1. Anchored by purpose instead of goals.
2. Characterized by values and principles instead of a selfish agenda.
3. Focused on leading with the heart instead of ego.
4. Concerned with cultivating long-term relationships instead of transactions.
5. Committed to demonstrating excellence through self-discipline instead of imposing power and authority.

Considering this characteristic will make us embrace the fact that success comes when we receive the biggest return on intentions.

Authentic leadership positions Christian leaders as purpose-driven and empowerment agents.

Their divine mission is to connect and interact with those appointed to lead and transform their lives by increasing the level of morality, motivation, resilience, awareness of their God- given assignment, and fulfillment of their purpose. Their overarching responsibility is to grow their community by being authentic, moral, strategic, responsive, situational, detailed- oriented, servant leaders. (significant).

They lead with integrity, humility, and the realization that they do not know everything. They learn and grow from their experiences and the experiences and opinions of others. They are willing to adapt to situations and surroundings. They practice being flexible and invite change.

They strive in challenging situations. They are good stewards of the people and things God has placed in their lives. Thus, they see the people they lead as valuable to God and call out what is good and true about them.

They lead with a clear sense of purpose and inspire others to align their actions and goals with a greater mission or cause. They articulate a compelling vision and help individuals understand how their work contributes to the larger purpose or values of the organization.

They emphasize meaning, passion, and the positive impact of purposeful collective efforts, creating a sense of shared purpose and intrinsic motivation among their followers; all pointing to the characteristics of a purpose-driven Christian leader.

I truly believe that there is a God-given purpose within every leader waiting for release. Such presence involves knowledge, insight, skilled intuition, and experience, as well as trust in the overwhelming process of birthing.

Birthing means that you go through a waiting time, a restless time, and a period of growth and transformation. This can be the loneliest time of your life. As you begin to digest this, ask yourself:

Do I know who I am? Do I know what it means to be a Christian leader in a professional space?

In my view, a purpose-driven leader is someone guided by God to discover his or her true self, distinct gifts, talents, and tasks. He or she utilizes these purposefully and deliberately to lead themselves and inspire others, drawing from their comprehension of their divine purpose.

This is a gradual process and can be painful and exhilarating. As a leader, you may experience fear, uncertainty, and numerous discouraging moments. Persevering through the loneliest times of your life can be tough but stay grounded. Stay true to your path. Take responsibility for yourself and what God has called you to do. Your purpose is established. You have been characterized by God and he has given you the key traits to succeed as a purpose- driven leader.

Characteristics of a Purpose – Driven Christian Leader

Dr. Janice Brooks, in her book, 'Purposefully Anchored', states that 'purpose is security for those who find it and an anchor for those who walk in it'. This very relevant and profound statement encapsulates the mindset and resolute stance of a purpose-driven Christian leader.

Purpose is the sure reference point and root of this type of leadership and leader. A purpose- driven leader usually manifests certain key traits based on individual motivations, inspirations, personal experiences, and the specific context in which they work. Seven basic characteristics or traits inspire these leaders to act as leaders namely:

Vision and Purpose

As a purpose-driven Christian leader, you have a clear and compelling vision rooted in your faith and moral and ethical integrity (personal leadership). You have a sense of purpose and direction for your organization and communicate this vision effectively to others (group leadership). Your vision is mostly aligned with the biblical rather than the worldly principles of leadership and your personal values, as you seek to bring about positive change and impact in the world. This vision and purpose serve as a driving force, motivating you to act and achieve your goals.

Authenticity and Alignment

As a purpose-driven Christian leader, you are true to yourself and your values. As a leader, you align your actions to all you are inside, your core self, personal relationships, career, and community. You are genuine and authentic in your leadership style. You are transparent about your weaknesses and struggles, allowing others to see your humanity. You have a deep faith in Jesus Christ and seek to live out your beliefs in all areas of your life. Your faith serves as the foundation for their leadership and decision-making. Your authenticity builds trust and credibility among your followers. This results in an overall success and personal well-being.

Learning and Growth

Additionally, as a purpose-driven Christian leader, you understand the importance of continuous learning, upskilling, personal and corporate growth. As a leader, you are motivated to act by a desire to grow in their understanding of themselves, others, God's purpose, and directions for your life. You also act to develop the skills and qualities necessary to effectively lead and serve others.

Impact and Contribution

As a purpose-driven leader, you are a model of excellence. You consistently demonstrate honesty, transparency, and accountability in your words and actions. Your character reflects a servant leader's heart, (which is a genuine desire to serve others). You prioritize the needs of your community or organization and seek to make a positive difference in the lives of those you lead.

You possess a deep sense of compassion and empathy for others. You consistently demonstrate your unconditional concern and care for the well-being and struggles of those you lead and are willing to walk alongside them, offering support, guidance, and understanding. You demonstrate love and kindness in your interactions with others. This desire to emulate Christ through this opportunity and role, to improve, and transform the lives of others, can be a powerful inspiration for action.

Overcoming Challenges

A purpose-driven Christian leader exhibits courage and boldness in their leadership. As a leader, you are not afraid to take risks or challenge the status quo when it aligns with your vision and biblical principles. You understand that challenges and obstacles are inevitable. You stand firm in your convictions and are willing to speak truth and advocate for justice, even in the middle of opposition.

Your belief in God's strength and empowerment, your self-assurance, and your grasp of your purpose motivate you to act.

Resilience and Perseverance

As a purpose-driven Christian leader you realize that leadership can be challenging, filled with abrupt turns and obstacle courses. You show resilience and perseverance in the face of adversity, relying on your faith and trust in God to sustain you through these difficult times. Your courage and determination allow you to face difficulties head- on and continue to work. You model resilience to inspire and motivate others to action.

Goal Achievement

As a purpose-driven Christian leader you understand the value of collaboration and teamwork. As a leader, you are open to actively seek input from others, value diverse perspectives, and foster a sense of unity and community among their team or organization. You foster inclusivity, and actively include others in decision-making.

Christian leaders may find that their vision and purpose drive them to seek learning and growth as they positively impact and contribute to the lives of others. While the desire to make an impact motivates them to overcome challenges and remain resilient and adaptable, they also remain true to themselves and their core values and align them to achieve desired goal.

Ultimately, the inspiration to action is deeply rooted in their relationship with God and their desire and commitment to please Him.

These characteristics work together to shape a purpose-driven Christian leader, committed to serving God, leading with integrity, and making a positive impact on the lives of others. As you reflect on this chapter, ask yourself:

How am I showing up? Do I know or understand the value I bring to the table?

Leadership Nugget

'Be a leader who is driven by purpose and not position nor power' – (Debasish Mirtha)

Let us pray:

Dear Lord,

Help me not to take my appointment for granted or my purpose lightly. Help me show up and represent you well as I respond to the needs around me guided and directed by you. Amen.

When you walk with purpose, you collide with destiny.

Chapter 5

The Wilderness Experience of Christian Leadership

If you faint in the day of adversity, your strength is small."

Proverbs 24:10

Defining the Wilderness Experience of a Christian Leader

In the previous sections, I have discussed my leadership journey, where I stand currently, and the lessons I have learned and am still learning. I have covered topics like defining leadership from a Christian perspective, understanding leadership anointing, appointment, commissioning, establishing a personal leadership style, finding a rhythm, and exploring the balance between leadership success and significance. We have also touched on the purpose behind leadership, different levels of assignments, and the distinct traits of Christian leadership.

I also presented the concept of consciously and intentionally birthing your purpose during a waiting period, a restless time, and a season of growth and transformation. Tucked snugly between this waiting period, and your growth and transformation, is what I called the 'wilderness of leadership'. Many leadership scholars refer to this as the crucibles of leadership.

I have learned that this is your divine preparation period. A period that puts you in a position where you cannot rely on others. A period where you have only yourself. It is when life and leadership put all your resources to the test. A period when you have to take responsibility for yourself and what God has called you to do, despite opposition.

Simply put, it is a spiritual warfare. During these times, you are desperate for a sign of God's favor.

I discovered that during this period, God is usually very near but very silent. He does not inform us ahead of time on the points of testing, what the test will be, and that he is behind all of this. He allows test after test to refine and shape us.

Undoubtedly, it can be excruciatingly painful when you do not recognize it for what it is. You can get restless and try to nudge the arm of providence. However, God's purpose or pruning cannot be thwarted. We have to surrender to overcome. It has to run its course. To come through this wilderness, we have to be devoid of any defensiveness, self-pity, victim mentality, and the tendency to manipulate the outcome.

It is after we have passed through to the other side that we recognize that he was there all the time, waiting patiently for us to complete our extraordinary preparation for the extraordinary tasks ahead.

Every effective leader goes through adversity. Hardship provides powerful lessons "about adapting and growing, about discovering new ways to engage or enroll others in a shared pursuit, and about recognizing the right thing to do and summoning the courage to do it" (Thomas, 2009, p. 22). "Not only so, but we also glory in our sufferings, because we know that suffering produces perseverance; perseverance, character; and character, hope." Romans 5: 3-5.

Contrary to common beliefs, genuine leadership is not a skill to acquire but a vulnerability that highlights our value, significance, and divine purpose. It is like learning to swim – we cannot do it on land; we need to immerse ourselves in water. Swimming in a pool is safer for non- swimmers than venturing into open waters like rivers or oceans.

Swimming in such environments is perilous due to the unfamiliar underwater currents and their interactions with our bodies. The dynamic nature of these currents can unexpectedly pull non-swimmers underwater, posing a serious risk.

This is the nature of a leader's wilderness experience. Every Christian leader is a non-swimmer until they are tried and tested and have experienced defining moments to master personal leadership. The Bible calls it 'self- control'.

We can never morally, authentically, and strategically lead people to successfully identify, understand, and complete their assignments if we are not able to do so for ourselves.

Authentic leadership, which is established as the life-blood of Christian leadership, is an understanding of personal identity, calling, and mission that only comes through 'God's own means to transform a leader's heart. God works in our lives to mold and strengthen us, to prepare us to be his leaders. Some experiences are excruciatingly painful. He orchestrates our experiences as challenges to mold our heart, to jar us out of our comfort zones, to shake up our complacency, to make us look inward, deep into our heart, until some crisis shows who we have become' (Seidel, 2008, p. 180).

I have learned that it is during this time of testing and hardship that you discover and cement your why, receive clarity, and discover a deep purpose regarding who you truly are, how powerful you are because of whose you are, whom you must take with you on your elevated stage and who are incapable of journeying with you.

It is at the end of this wilderness period and incredible survival that you can take on any challenge and emerge as a better and stronger amplified voice and anointed apostle of true leadership.

I particularly, love the way Seidel, (2008) & Moxley & Pulley (2003), sum this up. 'It is through difficult experiences that a Christian leader learns to depend on Christ, including the need to develop one's own sense of secure authentic identity (Seidel, 2008, p. 181).

Hardships provide "lessons about self- knowledge, sensitivity, control, and flexibility" (Moxley & Pulley, 2003, p. 14). Through hardship, leaders learn that they have limits (Moxley & Pulley, 2003, p. 15).

As leaders come to recognize their own limitation in controlling events, they also compassionately understand the limited control others hold (Moxley & Pulley, 2003, p. 15). For Christian leaders, the realization of their limitation/s should draw them to God and His sufficiency.

Identifying the Stages of the Wilderness Experience of a Christian Leader

Different scholars have different terms for what I describe as a leader's wilderness experience. Baraco (1997) identifies the wilderness experience as "defining moments," whose key elements consist of revealing, testing, and shaping.

Olivares (2011) describes it as "momentous events," "novel, vivid, emotional episodes that disrupt the continuity of daily life."

Horowitz and Van Eerden (2015) refer to it as "catalytic moments;" which lead to a reexamination of self-concept, a questioning of one's previously held perceptions of reality.

No matter the label, our task is to recognize it. This way, we will not overlook its ability to bring about transformation or to unveil character flaws and deficiencies that success might have hidden. As Christian leaders, addressing these issues become essential.

Thomas (2008) posits that every Christian leader encounter three 'wilderness' experiences throughout their career, namely: new territory, reversal, and suspension.

New territory refers to the early stages of your career in which you face unchartered waters, new territory, and the unknown. Reversals refer to the middle of your career and usually involve a period of success accompanied by severe loss or failure. Suspension is located towards the end of your career and can be characterized by loneliness and isolation. Each confronts the leader with particular challenges and tests the leader's resilience or adaptive capacity.

My initial experience in the beginning of my leadership journey in a professional space, was a baptism by fire of criticism, elevated expectations, confrontation, and offense. I was compared to the previous organizational leaders, as I struggled to acquaint myself with the community and organizational culture and started the drive for culture change.

Schein (1992), states that 'one of the major dilemmas that leaders encounter when they attempt to change the way organizations function is how to get something going that is basically countercultural, that does not fit the paradigm' (p. 140).

I came face to face with the complexity of culture and culture change and the peculiar problems of the organization I was called to lead. I had to pay keen attention to the numerous ways certain deep-rooted assumptions related to each other and how this pattern impacted the day to day behavior of all stakeholders.

The unknown elements did not reveal themselves easily or automatically. It took approximately four months into my leadership journey to realize that I was up against something much bigger than varying temperaments that I could later define as an informal structure or culture. The informal structure of any institution is more powerful than the formal structure and should never be underestimated.

An informal organizational structure is an 'organized' structure formed within a formal company without written guidelines.

However, it carries a powerful influence based on social norms and systems developed by members. There are no formal nor written rules, procedures, or chain of command. They grow through the day-to-day interactions between organizational members, which often arise based on interpersonal relationships and shared interests.

These individuals often come together due to shared interests, concerns, agendas, or grievances. Their loyalty to one another stems from a belief that this unity provides protection. Leaders within these informal circles are chosen based on personal qualities and their knack for guiding members toward a shared objective.

Unfortunately, negative information and rumors frequently circulate within these groups, fueling baseless conflicts and confrontations due to general assumptions. In essence, these members create a potent alliance capable of influencing leaders and shaping the fate of any institution, for better or worse.

There were numerous instances when things and persons confronted me as I grew into an understanding of the cultural assumptions of the institution. As I immersed myself in my new territory and the unknown, I had to constantly make logical inferences from what was presented to me. When I shared my logical inferences with the senior team, I was often stonewalled.

Over time it struck me that certain events that clearly appear incongruent from where I was standing, made sense whenever it was viewed through the lens of the existing organizational culture. I was constantly misunderstood. I became the most coveted popular offender at every level of the organization, internally and externally. From this vantage point, I discovered, but to date, do not clearly understand the structure and content of the various subcultures (informal structures) that existed.

Nonetheless, the impact of some of these subcultures became quite visible during the change process. This is because, I learned that almost every member of staff was related by blood, generation, marriage, or political affiliation and, through these passages to members of the community. This meant that if one person feels that they have been wronged, I was doomed.

Even if these individuals have not experienced mistreatment themselves, their perception holds immense weight. The perception they adopt can become their reality and resonate among loyalists at various levels. These loyal followers might subtly suggest that you have been overly stern or inflexible, without truly listening to both sides.

What is disheartening is that those who are expected to remain impartial often showcase their bias through their actions, body language, insinuations, and sweeping assumptions, influenced by their intent and allegiances. Unfortunately, they often communicate commands or directives with me, rather than engage in a genuine conversation.

During the initial months, another cultural assumption became evident; the double standards syndrome that permeated every level of the organizational structure.

Given that I was a forceful, outspoken individual, tact was a communication skill that I had to develop. Tact involves connecting and relating to the need of all stakeholders and being sensitive and careful in how I express myself to avoid offense and conflict.

As I sought to address double standards in a constructive and thoughtful manner, I was accused of being a hard taskmaster. I was repeatedly and deliberately misunderstood and misrepresented. Requests via my middle managers were often miscommunicated; there was an underlined suppression of important issues, ineffectiveness in decision-making, and an undesirable reinforcement of power imbalances.

To combat the blatant double standards syndrome that I inherited, I established transparent accountability mechanisms, prioritized humility and servant leadership, and promoted an open culture that encouraged dialogue and constructive criticism when necessary. I used the term 'painstakingly' because this problem had developed over several years but had not been identified as a crisis or issue that needed a resolution.

This culture encouraged individuals to accept that 'this is the way it has always been and could not be changed'. It was a mammoth task to get my staff to interrogate this issue, recognize its seriousness, and commit to do something about it. The result was a real sense of panic, distrust, and depression.

In a system or culture of friends, relatives, and comrades, middle managers can function symbolically as 'parent figures.' This can make it difficult for them to guide reform and propel people to shape up. In this context, group members find it very easy to blame each other and collectively avoid taking responsibility.

Consequently, during this period, everyone was on edge, and of course, I became the arch enemy.

In the midst of it all, as a leader, and particularly as a Christian, the bar of expectations is set exceedingly high. The weight falls on your shoulders to be everything to everyone – resolving issues in the blink of an eye, addressing longstanding problems overnight, fielding a barrage of questions (logical and illogical), meeting stakeholder demands, achieving exceptional outcomes, and propelling the organization into new realms of innovation and efficiency. This load can be overwhelming, especially without a robust support system.

Moreover, the commitment to uphold your fundamental values and integrity may lead to ethical quandaries that leave you feeling isolated. A leader's journey can sometimes feel lonely, as you strive to balance the myriad of demands while staying true to your convictions.

However, as was established, 'wilderness wisdom are curve balls that should drive Christian leaders to become more dependent on God and also more directed to be proactive problem solvers and learners.

Learning becomes more difficult as the rate of change increases because the solutions to the problems can only be derived from a pragmatic search for truth. As our problems change, so do our solutions and our desire for survival and improvement. One size will never fit all. As Christian leaders develop this mindset of mastery, overcoming, and determined resilience, they reap some desirable years of success before entering the next wilderness period that Thomas (2008), call reversals.

As I advanced through my leadership journey evolving as an overcomer and a survivor, victor instead of victim, I cultivated a growth mindset that allowed me and my team to reap 'seven years' of plenty. Systemic reform, community reform, and organizational reform took root and the benefits were widespread and celebrated by all stakeholders.

Additionally, I have honed specialized skills in leadership development, strategic planning, ethical leadership, capacity building, teacher training, coaching, and more. My journey has encompassed both successes and challenges, allowing me to secure sponsorships for infrastructure improvements, nurture emerging leaders, empower marginalized groups, and enhance student achievements. This multifaceted journey reflects my dedication to positive transformation and lasting impact.

I was also able to:

- Publish the findings of my research on disadvantaged rural schools on Amazon.
- Publish: research on small school leadership and presented a model (MISA) for improving student achievement in disadvantaged rural schools.
- Publish three Language Arts textbooks and workbooks that are being used in public schools in Jamaica and the Caribbean.
- Overcome many leadership challenges.
- Increase literacy and numeracy results by over 90%in six years.
- Revolutionize value-added education in small schools.
- Train and motivate numerous teachers to master the art of teacher and learning, classroom management and inclusiveness.
- Create a model for increasing student achievement in disadvantaged rural schools (MISA).
- Build capability and a community of practice via Healthy Relationship seminars for all stakeholders.
- Successfully designed and implemented numerous frameworks of accountability and performance matrix.
- Successfully coach, mentor, and a guide for stakeholders to help maximize their goals and accomplish set targets.

However, no matter how effective you are, it is part of the design of life for everyone to have highs and lows and inevitably face challenges and setbacks. In fact, the more effective and impactful you become, the more intense the wilderness experience. The difference between the new territory wilderness experience and the reversal wilderness experience is the type of tests.

During the wilderness experience labelled reversals, a Christian leader personally and professionally face intense personal attacks and challenges and an increase in specific leadership related issues. During this period, there is repeated unexplained loss and failure.

Additionally, the line between a personal crisis and a professional crisis is hardly distinguishable as the sources and implications of the crisis become locked or inseparable.

I am convinced that encounters with loss, grief, family crises, periods of stagnation, and spiritual struggles – whether in personal or professional spheres – possess a unique dynamic and dimension that sets them apart from other leadership challenges. They consume one's entire being and hold an unparalleled significance. Unfortunately, these phenomena are not widely comprehended or adequately addressed within the professional landscape.

I will never forget my experience of the last two years. I suffered personally and professionally. These were just not good years. It was a harsh wilderness season and a terrible leadership loneliness desert. This was the first time, but unbeknown to me, it would certainly not be the last. This was a highly emotional period in all areas of my life. During the three sixty-five days of each year of these two years, I had only two days, one for me and the other three sixty-four days against me. Things just got worse and worse. It was as if the universe was against me.

I encountered a relentless stream of crises, both personally and professionally. Grief weighed heavily as I faced sudden losses of immediate family members and students. Simultaneously, financial loss through account hacking added to the challenges. Amidst this, I navigated disappointments and unexpected conflicts. Team members resigned, some due to their own struggles, while others pursued new opportunities. The period was a true test of my resilience and strength.

I felt utterly defeated. Professionally, I carried out my role and met deadlines, but my grief made me oblivious to the silent critics who felt that because I was fulfilling my various roles, I was handling the heavy burden of grief and helplessness. No one looked beyond the role, to the human and the heavy sense of loss I was carrying. I was always expected to deliver effective leadership as if things were the same as before. I paid a high price. My body reacted. I got sick, disheartened, and depressed.

In our lifetime, we will experience multiple emotional storms. There are times we see the storm coming and brace for it. At other times, we will be completely caught off guard. Regardless of the situation, Christian leaders in their professional capacity must remember that during these crucial, desolate, and alone times, you are being pruned to produce.

Dealing with all of this caused me to reach a deeper level of awareness of God's call, my assignment, and His timing. I experienced a deeper connection and advanced to higher levels in my relationship with Him. I learned that these tests are crucial and reserved for a handful of leaders. I was carefully and divinely handpicked; purposefully commissioned.

If you are a Christian leader, there will come a day when the unthinkable and most unexpected happens to you either personally or professionally. I cannot tell you what will happen during this suspension period. It could be a painful separation or divorce, or you suddenly become the sole caregiver of an ailing loved one, despite the fact that you have capable siblings. It can be a huge betrayal from a business partner, trusted friend, or family member, or you may experience isolation and rejection from those who can, those you expect to, and who should be supporting you, or vindicating you.

This suspension period is marked by an unexpected turn of events, isolation and rejection, leadership specific situations, a spirit of accusation, betrayal or stagnation. In this heartbreaking moment, expect to have mostly miserable comforters, naysayers, and multiple accusers.

Your immediate questions will be, *Why is this happening to me? God! Why did you let this happen?* This period is the trickiest of them all.

You are solely tempted, and rightly so, to allow yourself to be filled with bitterness, hatred, and a desire for revenge.

Lanelle Harris (2010) describes this experience perfectly in one of his songs "BUT GOD' 'You are isolated and rejected. Your heart is breaking. The pain just comes in waves.

Everywhere you look, it seems like there is no peace. You try not to give up, but the tears will not relent. Any minute now, you might accept defeat. You stand there with impossible, the next word on your lips. Your vision has been blinded, and nothing makes sense. You look the whole world over for the meaning of it all, for the purpose in your pain. In the end, you will discover, there is no other answer; But God'

I experienced isolation and rejection as a leader in the most heartbreaking period of my life.

People who I have trained, empowered, modified, and enabled suddenly wanted me out of the way. They believed I had somehow received an overflow, had too much authority, restrained them too long, or done my time.

They felt it was now time to embrace the new and more rewarding culture you created and bask in the overflow of your glory; what I call the restlessness of empowerment and misinterpreted motivation.

Misinterpreted motivation occurs when those with second hand power refuse to wait their turn. As middle managers, they resent what they perceive as leadership leftovers. They cannot stand not being in their own spotlight. The idea of not living in their own glory consumes them. They yearn to be where you are, investing in a calling not meant for them. Paradoxically, their pursuit of greatness falls short not due to lack of effort, but from veering off their own path to fulfill someone else's purpose. In a symbolic sense, they parallel the prodigal son's sibling. As with that story, a price must be paid, something Christian leaders in a professional space must personally or professionally be prepared to face.

Experiencing a 'wilderness' phase toward the end of what might seem like a successful career can be profoundly distressing for those who fail to grasp the intricate interplay between human perceptions and the divine plans, authority, and power of God.

They are confusing success with significance, which was highlighted in chapter 2. I have to agree that not all leadership wilderness experiences end well. However, every Christian leader who, in all these circumstances, rely on clarity from God, spiritually interprets the direction and leading of God, and who surrenders the wills, passions, hurts, bitterness, disappointments, betrayals, accusations, conflicts, and confrontations to God's purpose, will find the golden nugget that God has placed in their overcoming.

We discover that these steps are ordered by God to voluntarily or involuntarily separate us from false success and present before us the true meaning of success, which is significance. What appears to be an undesirable end is a well- orchestrated transition for God. I know because after my wilderness experience I am still here.

Nothing and no one could take me out. God was not ready. Everything that happened turned out for my good. He allowed it for my perfecting of character. I am wiser and stronger. I am an overcomer.

So how do I know when I am in my leadership 'wilderness' experience?

Unmistakable Signs of a 'Wilderness' Experience

It must be clearly understood by every Christian leader that your wilderness experience is a spiritual warfare. For you do not wrestle against flesh and blood, but against principalities, against powers, against the rulers of the darkness of this age, against spiritual *hosts* of wickedness in the heavenly *places-(Ephesians 6:12).*

As was discussed in chapters 1 and 2, you were anointed, appointed and purposefully commissioned to fulfill a divine calling and assignment. The moment God appointed you the devil started paying attention to you and began planning his attack. This attack is not a football game for which you practice or train. It is not an exercise regimen from which you can opt out at any time. It is more like a long-distance race for those who can endure to the end.

True victory and triumph lie in conquering internal battles – the struggles of status and identity. This entails shedding defensiveness, self-pity, and the need for vindication. In essence, winning this inner battle requires comprehending your own limitations, acknowledging your dependency on God, and maintaining unwavering courage and focus on your calling.

While God appears silent and distant during this period, He does not leave us in the dark. As a Christian leader, there are some distinctive signs that can help you identify your wilderness experience.

These are:

You begin to doubt God working in your life and affairs. Your faith is sorely tested and tried. You feel that somehow God has abandoned you.

You begin to lose your hunger and passion for God. You pray less, study God's words less. All these desires seem to be suddenly removed. You lose your desire for spiritual fellowship.

You become fearful in ways that you have never experienced in the past. You have an irrational feeling or anxiety or fear of the future.

You suddenly become forgetful. You forget dates, important tasks, assignments, and appointments.

You become confused and disoriented. Things that were previously crystal clear to you become suddenly muddled and confusing.

During such times, you might find yourself revisiting past errors, hurts, and disappointments. It is easy to become consumed by thoughts of how others have wronged you, how they are hurting you now. This fixation can obscure your perspective, preventing you from recognizing the blessings God has granted you, the ongoing work in your present, and the potential He holds for your future.

Your emotions are out of whack. There is a sense of discouragement or being defeated. You suddenly feel worthless, helpless or hopeless.

Your sleep is under attack. You suddenly suffer from insomnia, sleep apnea, sleep paralysis, or can only take catnaps.

If you experience four or more of these signs you are having a wilderness experience.

However, as I conclude this chapter, I want you to keep in mind that after a wilderness experience, 'you emerge stronger, more engaged, and more committed than ever' Thomas (2008) to your calling and purpose. Our endurance is bound to a combination of spiritual discernment, overcoming and faith, that is, the ability to grasp context and purpose for your pain. 'These attributes allow leaders to grow from their 'wilderness' experiences, instead of being destroyed by them—to find opportunity where others might find only despair. This is the stuff of true leadership' (Thomas 2008, p. 4).

As you reflect on this chapter, ask yourself these questions:

Am I facing my wilderness experience? Why does one leader overcome their wilderness experience, and another is overcome?

Who are the players in the wilderness experience?

'Adversity shakes the foundation of our character to see if what we believe, and value is really worth standing for' – Rae Smith

Let us pray:

Dear Lord,

Lord thank you for being my guide and master player in my personal, professional, and emotional storms. Although I do not see, I know you carried and is still carrying me towards my divine destiny. I trust you and know you are working everything for my good. In Jesus' name, Amen.

Chapter 6

Rewards of the Wilderness Experience

'No discipline seems pleasant at the time, but painful. Later on, however, it produces a harvest of righteousness and peace for those who have been trained by it'. (Hebrews 12:11-13).

I discussed in Chapter 5 the personal and professional pains and lessons of the wilderness experience, but there is a calm after every storm. In this chapter, I discuss the benefits that a Christian leader receives after a wilderness experience. So far, you have learned that we cannot rush, manipulate or adjust the process God uses for our elevation. You do not lose when you are knocked down. You lose when you do not get up. It is not about what we pour in, but rather what we draw out. You cannot simultaneously be both the driver and the passenger, the student and the teacher, or the leader and the follower.

The overarching point is as a leader, you are expected to lead people. You may feel hard- pressed, crushed, broken, and perplexed, but not in despair. You may feel struck down, or abandoned, but you are not destroyed. You have also learned that if you overcome your wilderness experience, if you pass all the tests, you emerge stronger, more engaged, and more committed than ever' Thomas (2008).

You have learned that our endurance is bound to a combination of spiritual discernment and faith. That is, the ability to grasp the context and the purpose for your experience. 'These attributes allow leaders to grow from their 'wilderness' experiences, instead of being destroyed by them—to find opportunity where others might find only despair. This is the stuff of true leadership' (Thomas 2008, p. 4).

When you emerge from your wilderness experience, it is a divine call to ascend to the next level. You are being carried into a season of repositioning and a divine system of shifting and great transitioning. The thing about divine favor is that sometimes it looks like a disaster.

Joseph's journey to becoming second in command to Pharaoh began amidst a famine, and Daniel's path to becoming a respected figure in Nebuchadnezzar's court started with his captivity. The Lord often utilizes our trials and tribulations to release us from misguided pursuits and redirect us away from misplaced allegiances and superficial attachments.

False loyalty means being loyal in ways that go against God's intended loyalty: such as being loyal to people, mindsets, beliefs systems, policies, standards and organizations. By introducing you to abandonment, loneliness, rejection, and isolation, God uses your wilderness experience to challenge you to His fear and walk you into your purpose and assignment in the correct dimension.

False sentimentality is an emotional attachment to your job and specific persons in your organization. It can also refer to unnecessary fear and guilt over apologizing for being too nice.

False assignments are callings that you pour into but were never meant for you. These assignments drain our energy and pull you into seasons of unhealthy exhaustion and tiredness. As a result, you get distracted from your meaningful and purposeful commission. Your wilderness experience helps you put it all together. Difficult situations reveal who you really are, and the true heart of people.

Discipline can be tough to endure in the moment, but it yields a peaceful harvest of righteous living for those who embrace its training. The fact is, the harvest in your life is tied to your wilderness experiences, and the discipline you received, endured, and cultivated.

Your wilderness experience has now become your greatest weapon of enlightenment, decision-making, divine selection, and action.

You are clear about what is false and what is true; who is fake and who is genuine; whom you can take with you, and whom you must leave behind.

Only the right place can value you the right way. You can be the complete package but end up at the wrong address, and sometimes, we find that we are comfortable in the wrong place and get upset because we are not being valued. That is the single most important reason why we must ensure we correctly understand, identify, respond, and claim the rewards of our wilderness experience.

Understanding the Rewards of Your Wilderness Season

If you are standing on the other side of your wilderness experience or leadership crisis, you would have discovered that there are no finish lines. You either get tired and just stop, walk away without looking back, or get back on the horse and keep riding.

Regardless of your circumstances, remember that purposeful walking leads to destiny. In simpler terms, your wilderness experience shapes and readies you for where God wants you to make the greatest impact. After this journey, your purpose becomes clear.

I can tell you that after my leadership crisis, I asked several questions – *'What are the rewards in all of this? How do I know that God has closed this door and opened another? Where is/are the door/s that God has opened?* As I share the answers to these questions, it is important to note that they are grounded in my own wilderness experiences and leadership crisis, which is the framework of my understanding.

God uses unequaled and unique wilderness experiences in our lives to prepare us for elevation. Undoubtedly, your experience will be different from mine. However, some common patterns or details help us to identify the rewards, determine our response and how we claim our rewards.

Identifying, responding, and claiming rewards after a leadership crisis or wilderness experience requires a careful and strategic approach. Here are some common steps based on my experience, interpretation, research and pruning to help guide you through the process.

Identifying the Wilderness Rewards

Carolyne Njoku (2019) states that [our wilderness experience] 'are times in our lives when we experience circumstances that forever transform us. They challenge one to question their beliefs and values and leave one with a completely new identity' and might I add a new mindset. This is a distinctive mark of a wilderness reward.

I particularly love the way Njoku (2019) explains it. She notes that after a wilderness experience, the leaders "emerge in all their glory because they have confronted their worst fears, assumptions, beliefs and values" in that difficult moment. When we choose and seek to understand the meaning, purpose, and lessons from our wilderness experience, we become teachable, open-minded, adaptable, and possibly transformed. Humility, curiosity, resilience, and a willingness to learn, clothe our new identity and epitomize leadership.

Another distinctive mark is that you are not able to understand what God's plan is, but there is something that convinces you that God is up to something new. Although you are not sure exactly what it is or even if it involves a change in your place of serving, you just know that God is leading you into the divine. You have an unexplained urge to heed the call. You tap into a deep and abiding calling with a new and transformed mindset, energy, and charisma that is undefiled, pure, and new. This yielding can be very scary. After all, you are being taken into unchartered waters.

Throughout and after each wilderness experience, I heard a chorus of voices - the skeptics, the solitary encouragers, and the voices of destiny's helpers. What is remarkable is that, both overtly and subtly, they all echoed the same sentiment: 'God is at work,' 'let's see what emerges from this,' 'change is on the horizon,' 'we'll either emerge stronger or weaker,' and 'what doesn't break you, makes you.' Notably, some things did indeed change; me, my perspective, my mindset, cultivated habits, behaviors, motives for leadership, interpretations, as well as my personal and professional goals and priorities. Moreover, I influenced some people and circumstances in turn.

The other distinctive mark is that you grow into new depths of trust abandonment and rejection. As highlighted in the previous chapter, this is one crucial feature of your wilderness experience. When you come through your leadership crisis, you understand the complexity of rejection and the lessons it has taught you.You become a worthy agent because you are an honored subject.

Rejection and abandonment might not be your preferred way or being disrupted, but it can become a learning curb for us to bounce back and step into our purpose. None of your goals and opportunities come to you at once in your life.
Rejection provides valuable insights into areas we can enhance. It prompts us to assess what is

changeable and what is not, guiding us onto new and intriguing journeys. In essence, rejection serves as both a mender and a preparer.

Then there is the confirmation in your spirit. After your struggle with self and wrestle with the difficulty of the mirage of voices and unsolicited consultants, you finally surrender to where God is leading you, and accept the will of God from a deep and resounding confirmation in your spirit.

You know you have made the right decision and chosen what is best for you.

"For me, it pushed me to pursue my lifelong dream of becoming a full-time transformational strategic Christian leadership, life coach, trainer, and consultant.

I obtained my certification in 2015, but until recently, I only engaged in life coaching part- time through direct informal referrals, often without charging. This experience underscored my deep-seated passion for offering support, mentorship, and guidance and my divine mandate for justice and advocacy. It fueled my desire to empower Christian leaders in a professional space, especially women, to overcome the unique challenges they face, especially in the toughest times.

The final distinctive mark is to understand that opportunities come from seemingly nowhere.

These transitions may catch you by surprise, but they are not unexpected to many others. You have amassed various experiences to prepare you for this higher level of assignment, and your distinct skills and talents perfectly align with your new identity. However, you remain adaptable, recognizing that you are under the divine anointing and appointment described in Chapter 1, realizing that you are intentionally appointed and purposefully commissioned for this purpose.

Accepting Your Wilderness Rewards

One of the questions you ask yourself after a wilderness experience is *'what could I have done anything differently to avoid this experience?* This is a natural response, but that is not the question that we should ask. Our wilderness experience tests our capacity for leadership.

While rewards may come after successfully navigating a crisis, it is crucial to remain vigilant and proactive in identifying and addressing potential issues.

The questions that we must then ask is 'What *are the lessons that I needed to learn and/or what are the lessons that I have learnt that I need to enable me going forward?*

Recovering from a wilderness experience or leadership crisis is a journey that requires patience, resilience, and dedication. Our immediate response should be one of reflection, investigation, and contemplation.

The first step is to use the crisis as a learning opportunity for exemplifying Christian leadership. God permits every wilderness experience to refine us. Discipline, as previously noted, can be initially painful, but for those who undergo its training, the rewards are ultimately sweet and peaceful.

Your response must be seen, crafted, and delivered in that spirit. Bear in mind that your response should be from a surrendered rather than a resisting place as it can either make or break you. How we receive our rewards is crucial. We can be either resistors, receivers, or controllers.

If you adopt a resistor mode, you may have an overwhelming desire to be vindicated, award blame, adopt a victim mentality, and wallow in self-pity. You may be tempted to resist this divine pruning for various reasons, such as a fear of the unknown, a loss of control, or the perceived negative impact on your interests or routines. People close to you, both in personal and professional spheres, may react to the crisis with resistance fueled by anger, shame, disbelief, or a profound awareness of the unvarnished truth.

They may even be vocal in their resistance because they are ignorant of the divine turn of events and orchestration of God's plan for your life-changing pivot. They may also express their resistance by asking you to compromise your values, truth, and beliefs.

I distinctly remember during the peak of my leadership crisis, being advised to apologize to individuals whom I had no prior interaction with or had caused no harm to. Additionally, I was encouraged to apologize to others for matters related to my diligent and unwavering adherence to our organization's established policies and standards, since stakeholders believed I could have handled them more agreeably.

There were numerous times I was thrown under the bus so that the forest of accusation could be cleared, and the so-called mediators could convince themselves that they had amicably resolved an undesirable issue and move on with the business of the organization.

Another supporter empathetically explained how this situation could hinder my progress and tarnish the remarkable achievements I had garnered on my leadership journey. They emphasized the importance of considering the seemingly irrational and baseless demands of the discontented, whose grievances were largely fueled by unfounded rumors and unsubstantiated claims.

The spotlight was on me. However, the morale of my team was drastically reduced, and team members became cautious, apprehensive, defensive, angry, disengaged, and demotivated. Emotions were on the edge.

As a Christian leader or any leader for that matter, handling your emotions and the emotions of your team players and stakeholders, while adjusting and trying to make sense of the crisis or what had occurred, can become extremely distressing. You are placed between a rock and a hard place. The truth is you can buckle under the heavy burden or remain strong–focused and steadfast- knowing that this experience is profitable for your learning, reproof, correction and instruction. So, you can be thoroughly furnished unto all goods works.

During these times, resisting is the worst thing that you can do. As a leader, you are expected to lead in times of plenty and famine. When you understand that the nature of your wilderness experience is symbolical of a spiritual warfare, you identify the root cause of the crisis and the nature of the impact on you, your team morale, and your organization. Regardless of the circumstances, it is imperative to assist them in overcoming their challenges and guide them toward success.

If you are in controller mode, your only desire is for your wilderness experience to go away. You may want to take decisive action and remove the leaders responsible for the crisis. You may be tempted to decide with speed over precision to rapidly determine what matters most. You may be tempted to slacken and adjust established measures, policies, and standards of control to ensure ongoing operations and maintain current functions.

Consequently, interests and priorities may clash, and emotions and anxieties run high as you try to reach consensus on urgent matters. Given the presence of deceitful individuals, hidden agendas, and the silence of those who know the truth, it is understandable to develop a sense of mistrust towards others. This might lead to a tendency to take on all responsibilities yourself. Alternatively, you may choose to adopt a more assertive leadership style to maintain control and curb perceived chaos resulting from a perceived power vacuum.

You may appoint new middle managers and change your communication channels. You create a narrative that insists on transparency and the truth, and drill down into your accountability matrix. You might find yourself carefully selecting who sits at the table and who you keep at a distance.

I have discovered that this leadership crisis management mode is particularly unhealthy after a wilderness experience for these reasons. It not only serves to widen the gap between the perceived disgruntled and the leadership, but also drives fear and uncertainty into team players, creating additional mistrust and confusion, and increasing miscommunication.

In my experience, in the controller mode there are no clear benefits or value to individuals, and it only serves to strengthen the misconception of the technocrats that a leadership crisis can only be resolved via a required increase in effort and skill.

Controlling people and circumstances out of bitterness, malice, or revenge is never a desirable catalyst for restitution or growth in any organization. None of us can manipulate or control the outcomes of a divine order. All our times and seasons are in God's hands.

I recommend that rather than attempting to exert control or dictate outcomes after a wilderness experience, strive to comprehend and address the perspectives and concerns of stakeholders through open communication, deliberate engagement, and support. Cultivate compassion and empathy for both yourself and others. Learn to manage and embrace all your emotions, and assist others in doing the same

If you opt to embrace the role of a receiver, you acknowledge that your current development has prepared you for your present position in a way that other paths may not have.

You rise above defensiveness, self-pity, and alterations of manipulation at all levels. You open yourself to learn things God has taught and will continue to teach you. You want to grow, adapt, and be transformed into who God created you to be.

You are among the obedient, teachable, and surrendered group of movers and shakers. A qualified overcomer molded and fashioned for service, purposefully commissioned for excellent work. In this role, you recognize that you are not the ultimate master of your destiny; rather, it is in God's hands. Therefore, you actively listen for and follow His divine guidance. You also embrace the understanding that His intention is to bless you, your endeavors, and shower you with abundance and growth.

You understand that your seedtime has passed, and it is time for God's harvest. You recognize that you are set in place by a force that is immovable, and doors are now opened that no human hands can shut.

You will receive your reward when you are to be rewarded. No one can stop what God has planned for you. Giving always precede receiving. Receiving is not an obligation; it is a reward. Things are working in divine order. Your wilderness season came first and your reaping time after. When you open yourself to receive from God after your wilderness experience, your hope will not be in vain.

Claiming Your Wilderness Reward

After successfully identifying and responding to your wilderness experience, you now need to claim the benefits and rewards of your efforts. To claim these rewards as a Christian leader, you have to ensure that you hold no grudges.

You must also resist any inclination to say any hurtful or evil thing to the players in your wilderness experience.

The truth is, they were caught off guard as what they thought would bring your downfall actually became your elevation. Your response should be to reject evil and nurture goodness, aligning your actions with what God would approve.

You must listen and do all that God asks, and get your divine assignment/s done, and ensure that they are done well. You must acknowledge the fact that you are still here. The wilderness experience came and went. It left you here. You are a victor, not a victim.

You are a conqueror. You were not conquered. There was a purpose in your pain and a message in your mess. You became vulnerable, yet you are more valuable.

Claim victory in your vulnerability. Rid yourself of defeating actions, lingering remorse, and miserable comforters. They only drag you down and take you back to that place God has successfully carried you through.

Resist negative thoughts and limiting beliefs. Looking back is not the answer. Your wilderness experience has passed. You have the advantage, act upon it. By taking these steps, you emerge stronger, more resilient, and fully prepared for future challenges.

As you reflect on what you learnt in this chapter, ask yourself these questions:

How do I regain confidence as a Christian leader in a professional space after a wilderness experience? How do I lead with dignity? What are the mistakes I must avoid going forward?
Leadership Nugget:

Being challenged in life is inevitable. Being defeated is optional'- Power of Positivity'

Let us pray:

Dear God,
Help me learn the lessons you want to teach me through my pain because I know that in the end it will be for my good and your glory. I shake the spirit of remorse and resistance, so I can receive bountifully from you and carry out my God- given duties without fear or favor and fulfil your purpose.

Amen

Chapter 7

Leading with Dignity After Your Wilderness Experience

'For kings and all who are in authority – 1 Tim.2:2, clothe yourself with eminence and dignity, honor and majesty – (Job 40;10). In all things show yourself to be an example of good deeds, with purity in doctrine, dignified'- (Titus 2:7).

So far, we have learned that secular leadership and Christian leadership have commonalities and differences; that Christian leaders in a professional space embrace a dual identity of Christian and professional. We have also learned that Christian leadership acknowledges and accepts the paradigm that leadership is a ministry, understand that it is God appointed and purposefully commissioned, and that core values cannot be separated from your God given assignment, leadership styles, and divine purpose.

We have accepted that wilderness experiences or leadership crucibles carry an anointed transformation, transitioning, repositioning, and elevation that confirm a purposeful commission. Doors are opened that no one can shut. You can choose to enter with dignity or hang back in shame, remorse, or self-condemnation.

There is no doubt that a wilderness experience can be emotionally charged and challenging for everyone involved and how you respond as a leader can have a significant impact on the wellbeing, confidence, productivity, recovery and morale of yourself, your team, and organization. As a leader, there may be times when you need to take a voluntary or involuntary leave of absence to manage the overwhelming surge of emotions, both internally and externally.

However, there are also instances where you can navigate these challenges with wisdom, integrity, dignity, and authority, ultimately regaining the trust and respect of your team and stakeholders.

Leading with grace and dignity following a wilderness experience or leadership crisis is a vital element of Christian leadership.

Leading with grace requires a combination of emotional intelligence, empathy and compassion, and a commitment to growth. It requires resilience, humility, strong decision- making skills, and the willingness to consider multiple perspectives and options.

Leading With Grace Utilizing Emotional Intelligence

In this context, emotional intelligence entails a personal commitment to enhance self-awareness and cultivate mindfulness. It involves mastering the ability to respond thoughtfully rather than react impulsively to challenging situations, emotions, and comments.

It is the ability to navigate your emotional responses that include how you present yourself to the world, what you say, how you say, what you say, and how the world perceives you. It also points to self-regulation and self-efficacy, as you pay attention to understanding what, when, and how you are triggered.

It is important to note that emotional intelligence is not about being able to mitigate problems, handle confrontations, shouting matches, accusations, or being a doormat. It is more about the ability to manage and regulate your emotions, being wise as a serpent, knowing when to step into these confrontations, when to deal with the accusations, when to be silent, when to lovingly but boldly stand your ground, and how to enter these situations having the proficiency and ability to find common ground and rapport.

It is also helping and supporting team members to identify and confront their emotions, recognize their triggers, and acknowledge the concerns and experiences of those affected by the wilderness experience. It involves giving constructive feedback instead of personal criticism, and challenging behaviors rather than people.

I vividly remember my own wilderness experience as a leader, where I delved deeper into my inner self. I consciously tuned out the cacophony of external voices and withdrew into a profound state of introspection. There were decisions I had to make that I should have made long before. There were emotions I acknowledged, examined, and realistically placed into the growth, development, and productive spaces of my leadership cabinet. I embraced all these emotions as valid, sorting them into their respective leadership files. I made a conscious choice not to harbor unnecessary emotions, channeling my focus solely on those that were nurturing and capable of fostering personal growth.

I had numerous one-on-one group sessions to help team members examine, recognize, understand, and act on their emotions. This mutual understanding ultimately controlled how team members later worked together, communicated, and treated each other.

Utilizing Empathy and Compassion

This refers to the deliberate effort that you make as the leader to get over yourself and not take anything personally. As you strive to put self aside and listen to the concerns, fears, anxieties, and the exchange of loyalties, you demonstrate genuine empathy and understanding to create a safe place for people to be themselves.

This does not mean that you are blindly agreeable. As a leader, you must understand your team member's point of view and be assertive or firm when they use this accommodation to attempt to run you over. As you mindfully focus on using facts and logic and not emotions, you need to calmly have that difficult conversation. This approach involves meeting team members and stakeholders at their current level and assisting them in reaching higher, all while fearlessly engaging in difficult conversations. The goal is to facilitate productive discussions that lead to positive outcomes, all the while upholding one's dignity.

Leading with Dignity

Leading with dignity means that you first learn to understand and lead yourself before you endeavor to lead others. Taking care of yourself after a major setback is paramount to leading yourself. Ensure that you have the resources and support you need to cope with the stress and demands of leadership during these challenges' times.

Wilderness experiences create a major discomfort for the leader. However, acknowledging that God meant it for your good, allows you to recognize that you have a thought partner, support partner, confidant, sounding board and supportive voice of reason when you need it the most. If you surrender and trust the process by leading yourself with dignity, you get to where God is taking you faster.

Leading yourself means you have the courage to stand up for what is right. It means communicating assertively to make sure your needs are met without using manipulation, aggression, or compromising your core values. It also means that you have the insight and capabilities to achieve your personal and professional God-given assignment and mandates. It is the capacity to first comprehend yourself and then apply that understanding to ensure that each team member is afforded the right to maintain his or her dignity.

Leading with dignity entails actively advocating for a team member's entitlement to respect, value, and honor. As a leader, you take steps to protect their reputation and boost their self- esteem. You acknowledge their abilities, unique qualities, and talents, refraining from actions that might undermine them. You demonstrate respect for their actions, potential, individuality, and contributions.

Utilizing Humility

During and after the wilderness experience, I have learned that the leader and team members may display feelings of uncertainty and anxiety. They are uncertain about the future of the organization, their roles, and the stability of their jobs. This uncertainty can lead to increased anxiety and stress. Leaders and team members can overcome by exercising humility. Sharing concerns, being honest about challenges and progress, focusing on what you can control, maintaining open communication with one another and seeking support from colleagues help alleviate anxiety and gradually rebuild trust.

Ensure that you lead by example. Demonstrate the values you want to see into your team.

Modelling resilience, even from a distance, gradually adapting and accepting change, and unpretentiously cultivating a positive attitude as you navigate through this post crisis period, cement your commitment to uphold the dignity and well-being of yourself and your team.

Building Resilience

I have also observed that during a wilderness experience or leadership crisis, there is a lack of clear direction and guidance from the leader.

When a leader is feeling disoriented or overwhelmed, he/she often requires time to regroup and process the numerous surprises and unexpected developments. This situation can leave team members feeling disoriented themselves, uncertain about their objectives and priorities.

A team member usually has to be selected, internally or externally by default to pick up the slack. Team members are then encouraged to come together to set common goals and create a sense of purpose. Collaboratively identifying key tasks and milestones can help keep the team aligned and focused on moving forward to building resilience.

A wilderness experience can also erode trust between leaders and team members, making it challenging to work together effectively.

Rebuilding trust takes time and effort from all parties involved. Being consistent in actions and communication, delivering on promises and purposefully, and intentionally moving forward despite undesirable circumstances, goes a long way to build resilience.

Despite the challenges, a leadership crisis can present opportunities for personal and professional growth as team members adapt to new situations. Leading with dignity requires the leader to encourage and nurture a growth mindset within the team, where team members see challenges as opportunities for learning and development.

Encourage learning and growth. Reflect on the lessons learnt and the areas for improvement for future prevention. Make a deliberate effort to celebrate achievements and progress, no matter how small, to foster a positive outlook.

A wilderness experience can also negatively affect team morale and motivation. When team members lack confidence in their leader, they may become disengaged and less committed to their work. To overcome low morale, team members must be encouraged to reignite motivation by reinforcing their sense of purpose in their work and focusing on the impact they can make despite the crisis. Encouraging positive relationships and recognition among team members can also help improve motivation and build resilience.

Combining Strong Decision-Making Skills

One of the most obvious signs of leading with dignity after a wilderness experience is for a leader to take responsibility. That is taking ownership of the crisis and the consequences that resulted from it. The key is to avoid blaming others or deflecting responsibility. Instead, we must take the required actions to move forward and learn from the experience.

Set clear goals and priorities for the recovery process. It is highly important to communicate the path forward and establish a sense of purpose and direction for your team. This requires strong decision-making skills that only a few possess during this period of uncertainty and distraction. Consequently, productivity may suffer during a leadership crisis.

The leader, at this point, has to use strong decision-making skills to counter decreased productivity by setting clear goals, prioritizing tasks, and breaking larger projects into smaller and manageable steps. They also have to make the unpopular and burdensome decisions to provide the means and support needed by each team member to maintain productivity. I describe this situation as both unpopular and challenging because after a crisis, the task of enhancing productivity can sometimes feel like an added burden, potentially overwhelming an already stressed team.

Consider Multiple Perspectives

In order to offer essential support while leading with dignity, a leader must cultivate a positive and inclusive atmosphere. During and after a wilderness experience, effective communication can falter, with critical information going unshared or rumors running rampant. A leadership crisis can exacerbate tensions among team members, particularly when there are conflicting viewpoints on how to address the situation. To prevent confusion and ensure clarity, the leader must take the initiative to be open and transparent in their communication, even when others may not.

Honesty and transparency are the cornerstones that preserve trust in your genuine leadership. Even if it results in adversity, you can stand before yourself and be confident in receiving God's scrutiny and approval. Moreover, you can take solace in the knowledge that those who follow in your footsteps will perceive you as faithful, and the path you've walked will inspire them to believe, while the life you've lived will encourage them to obey.

You can improve communication by being proactive in sharing information transparently and factually. It may also be helpful to establish regular team meetings or check-ins to ensure everyone stays informed. You must promote a culture of inclusion, where everyone's contribution is valued and respected. To overcome any team or stakeholder conflict, it is essential to promote open dialogue and active listening.

Encourage team members to voice their concerns and work together to find common ground. In situations where a consensus cannot be reached, mediation or the involvement of a neutral third party may become necessary, particularly in severe cases.

During a leadership crisis, teamwork and mutual support among team members are crucial. Leading with dignity promotes quality engagement starting from the top down. It produces a healthier work environment, lower stress, improved wellbeing, and quality engagement, performance, and productivity. It provides a psychosocial safety net that is fundamental for inclusion, meaning and purpose. It's a net in which individuals can be themselves, voice concerns, and be heard.

By communicating openly, staying resilient, and working together, teams can navigate through difficult times and emerge stronger. God tests and assesses us through the ordinary events of life. It's often the small things or crisis that unveil the true nature of one's heart (White, 1844).

Leading with dignity means you will manifest unbending integrity. Deceptive tactics and dishonest dealings, often used to further personal interests, are viewed as abominable by God. When as a leader you are genuinely connected with God, it becomes evident in your life. Your actions align with the teachings of Christ, and you refuse to compromise your honor for personal gain. Your principles are firmly grounded, and your behavior in worldly matters reflect those principles.

Firm integrity shines forth as gold amid the dross and rubbish of the world. You may be lied on, talked about, plotted against, ridiculed, and even make huge leadership mistakes, but you still win. In the end, your integrity speaks for itself and the truth cannot be ignored. 'Through all things, you are more than a conqueror, through him that loved us' – (Romans 8:37).

As you reflect on this chapter, ask yourself these questions: *As a Christian leader do I lead with dignity and grace? What are the mistakes I should avoid? How do I create an organizational culture that brings out the best in me and my team players?*

Leadership Nugget:

"Lead from the back and let others believe they are in front"- Nelson Mandela

Let us pray:

Dear Lord,

Grant me discernment, strength, and resolve to lead with integrity, compassion, empathy, and dignity, even in challenging times. Help me listen, connect, and seek your guidance in every decision, so I can be a humble servant, bridge and light as I lead. Amen

Chapter 8

Leadership Misunderstandings

'Watch carefully how you live. Not as persons who do not know the meaning of life, but as someone who is wise. Do not continue in ignorance but try to understand what the will of the Lord is'- (Ephesian 5: 15.16).

In the previous chapters, we learn that:

Christian leaders are anointed, appointed, and purposefully commissioned by God.

Your various assignments and trials in the wilderness were not haphazard occurrences; they are divinely orchestrated and carry a significant purpose.

Your leadership role is not without profound meaning. It has been meticulously designed to be an integral part of a larger cosmic plan, carefully crafted by God. While these experiences and responsibilities may not have been devoid of challenges, God permits them to mold, nurture, and prepare you for a unique and invaluable role in God's grand design.

It is something that is not about you, but bigger than you. It intimately involves you and makes you what God created you to be; a purpose driven leader.

We also accept that an understanding of this gives our life focus, honorable simplicity, eternal weight and peace, and our service meaning, resulting in a life of significance.

It is often communicated that the way you define leadership defines your leadership. I have learned from my leadership journey that leadership rests on two pillars; speculation and revelation.

These are the two lenses through which leadership is perceived and defined.

The most popular is Speculation.

Many expert leaders theorize and make absolute statements about leadership, trying to explain it by categorizing positions, leadership types, and tasks. They see effective leadership as making people do what they should to achieve organizational goals.

These concepts hold expectations that immortalize leadership with numerous misconceptions, often converting talented leaders into blind guides fumbling in the dark searching for the leadership light.

Langer (1987) calls this state as 'mindlessness,' which is a mindset that applies yesterday's business solutions to today's problems.

The other concept is Revelation. Revelation for me has a twofold capacity, and for this reason, I have great admiration and respect for it. As mentioned earlier, I accepted the reality that many of the things that I studied, read, and was schooled in regarding leadership could only be generally applied but not smoothly translated and pragmatically used in my leadership setting or context without modification and adaptation.

The other side of revelation is embedded in the knowledge and understanding of what purposefully commissioned leadership truly looks and feels like in this temporary symbolic organization called life. It is about accepting the things that you cannot change; having patience as you are prepared and pruned for each level.

Demonstrating faith and courage to endure and withstand what you cannot understand. While speculation often seeks one-size-fits-all solutions, revelation shows that leadership is an active and dynamic force, an ongoing journey rather than a final destination.

Outside of this context, misunderstandings about leadership become prevalent and can result in ineffective leadership practices and outcomes. These ineffective practices may include leaders seeking excessive external approval, experiencing burnout due to unrealistic expectations, harboring resentment and anger, and engaging in behaviors like nepotism, cronyism, and unhealthy competition, that are sometimes mistaken for signs of leadership success.

Common Misconceptions

Leadership is a position of authority and power. When we define leadership based on speculation, we conclude and respond to leadership as a position of authority or power, where the leader always has the last word, and the authority to delegate.

A position of authority where micromanagement and stringent control of every detail are the norm, with everything needing approval from a single source. A position from where you demand immediate compliance instead of command loyalty and respect, and has a modus operandi that says, 'Do as I tell you', accompanied by a rigorous screening and requirements.

This definition is crafted on defensiveness and manipulation that rewards compliance to a chain of command rather than initiative, creativity, and effort. These conditions highlight one of the most significant misconceptions of leadership, which ultimately has a detrimental impact on the organizational climate.

Rajeev Peshawar (2019) says that speculation leads us to misinterpret followership for leadership. This ongoing confusion leads us to consistently promote and reward followership as if it were leadership.

On my leadership journey, I have had a few institutional-appointed, so-called 'coach and mentors,' who eloquently touted a principle of leadership based on an open-door policy that takes everyone into account, but modelled an authoritative, restricting, and smothering form of supervision. When judiciously examined, it became crystal clear that their idea of supervision (leadership) is an instrument of control that requires you to stick to the understood script, stay in character, or run the risk of being branded noncompliant, controversial, and unsupportive. In other words, the problem.

An intense scrutiny of repeated actions and 'skillful hypocrisy' revealed that shared leadership was a 'no-no' and distributing or balancing leadership was only mouth talk or seminar content presented by symbolic believers who are paid to present and mirror other men thoughts.

I quickly realized on my journey that most organizations in my industry were not viewed as a human community with unique individuals, histories, and stories, but rather a symbolic animal farm with the unwritten but well understood bargaining rights of proud 'slave catchers' who use wit to subtly promote the belief that:

All persons are equal, but some persons are more equal than others - (George Orwell).

One size fit all when the leader is careful to strategically align team members with the vision.

Square pegs can fit into round holes with creative maneuverings and quick fix solutions.

Best practices from other contexts can be adapted to your setting as a Band-Aid for desired results.

Stakeholders should not approve a new contextual, strategic direction without proven best practices.

This leadership approach, which is heavily steeped in speculation, is a game that very few leaders can win, and my thrust to eliminate this imbalance became a double-edged sword. I believe that it not only places a vice grip on creativity, innovation, appreciative inquiry, greatly decrease personal accountability, and responsibility, but also demand that you give shoes to people who have no feet.

Herein lies a leadership paradox. You must act in the best interests of those you lead without their studied input, but appreciative inquiry must be done to keep up appearances even if the information is stored. The fact is, appreciative inquiry was constantly recommended, but always ended up being a wild goose chase leading to a dead end, as it is really a smokescreen to pacify proactive leaders.

Many times, on my leadership journey, I sought guidance from the organization's technocrats when facing tough decisions for my team and the organization's best interests. However, I was reminded that as the leader and final accountable officer, it was ultimately my responsibility to persuade my team to align with the desired approach, even if it obviously conflicted with the technocrats' moral views or core values; another leadership paradox.

Another approach that can be equally impractical is that a leader must always aim for consensus. There have been numerous times when I tried getting consensus on crucial matters, and key stakeholders remained silent. This can be due to fear, misinformation, a silent critic, disengagement, disgruntlement, or uncertainty. Whatever the reason, it can be extremely frustrating for a leader. Leadership revelation informs us that while consensus is desirable and very valuable, it is not always feasible or necessary. Effective leaders have to make strong decisions when needed and must be prepared to give a rationale behind those decisions.

The fact is that as humans, we are not naturally cohesive or compliant, and so leaders are needed to provide guidance, inspire, motivate, and rally people around a common cause. Effective leaders centralize the vision and help pave the way for achieving departmental and organizational goals.

I remember a story that has left a lasting impact on me throughout my leadership journey. I often share it as an icebreaker during professional training and development sessions because it illustrates the point I want to convey.

There was an important job to be done. Everybody was sure that somebody would do it. Anybody could have done it, but nobody did it. Somebody got angry about that, because it was everybody's job. Everybody thought anybody could do it, but nobody realized that none would do it. It ended up that everybody blamed somebody when nobody did what anyone could have done.

Someone has to be at the wheel. Someone must guide the effective merging of expertise, talents, and strengths, and that person must be held accountable for helping and allowing people to become their best self.

Leadership guided by revelation provides a wonderful toolkit for authentic and authoritative leadership with a modus operandi that says, 'come with me'. In this context, leadership is more of a partnership than a position of power or authority. This translates into a long-term relationship, where the leader and group members are connected in such a way that the power between them is balanced.

Leadership is not a one size fits all as some technocrats advocate by their conflicting actions. Effective leadership adapts to different situations and contexts and require varying styles and approaches.

Revelation leads us to ponder on the ways we have unknowingly confuse and reward followership for leadership.

Persons should not lead at a certain age.

Another common misconception is the belief among many technocrats that individuals should not assume leadership roles at a certain age. Leadership speculation fosters a widespread assumption that has become ingrained in the professional world, suggesting that leadership loses its relevance as a leader ages, with the belief that older leaders become set in their ways and have diminishing significance beyond the age of fifty.

Consequently, there is an unwritten but understood resolution to discard or eliminate them.

Since 2015, I have observed that in many industries, recruiters prefer hiring 30- and 40- year old's, who presumably have 'fresh, new ideas,' creativity and out of the box thinking, instead of considering older adults with years of experience, creativity, patience, and expertise.

Driven by the misconception that performance worsens, and capacity decreases as people age, older employees are expected to just quietly fade into the background so that younger talent can take the reins. By all accounts, this often has a negative impact on the organization as most young leaders lack mentorship and the required respect for the expertise and wisdom that comes through experience.

Lack of expertise and improper guidance often places the organization on a merry-go-round of disgruntlement and disengagement, inefficient use of time and resources, and disillusionment on the part of the young leader who has not be mentored.

It is my strong and studied opinion that leadership is like fine wine. In fact, leadership revelation agrees that it gets better with age and experience. Succession planning provides a connection and mentorship that results in a smooth transition for young leaders and maintains harmony whilst safe guarding the dignity of the retiring leader.

I would never deny that there is a tendency in all leaders (young and old) to continue doing whatever has worked, as they settle into leadership. 'Certainty [deepens] and tends to develop with continued success' Langer (1987).

I would also have to agree that this approach can make them vulnerable to a fixed mindset. They may become resistant to change, thinking; "That is what works! That is how we've been doing it for the last five years, and it has yielded great results, so I see no reason to change it." I have learned that this can pose a significant challenge for team leaders in helping talented and intelligent team members transition and adapt to changing contexts, personalities, and norms. It can also be challenging to reframe false loyalties and sentimental attachments.

I believe that it is a fixed mindset and not age that is a key hindrance to effective leadership. There is no universally perfect age for leaders or leadership. Individuals can demonstrate effective leadership qualities such as authenticity, empathy, compassion, creativity, logical thinking, focus, innovation, and self-control at any age.

Additionally, different life experiences and angles can bring supreme wisdom and unique strengths to leadership roles. Some individuals have the natural tendency, divine anointing, appointment, and commission to develop these qualities at a young age. Others have to develop these qualities over time through experiences and learning, and quite often via a wilderness experience.

Revelation informs us that regardless of the individual's spectacular attributions, capabilities, connections, support partners, resources, unique gifts, and talents, everyone has to grow into leadership. Thus, it is more advantageous for any organization to focus on the proof of the needed skills, no matter who has them.

Men Make Better Leaders than Women

Another misconception based on leadership speculation is that men make better leaders than women, because they are less emotional and command more respect. When a female leader makes tough decisions that are necessary for the organization but prove unpopular among staff and stakeholders, she is often perceived as exhibiting masculine traits, acting out of character, or being highly respected but not necessarily loved. This perception arises from her prioritizing what is right over what is popular, rather than simply seeking to please everyone.

There have been times in my leadership journey, when I have had to make difficult decisions. I remained true to my core values of being just and honest and doing what was right more than what was popular. On these infamous occasions, I was described with great admiration as leading the institution like a man, making decisions like a strong man and holding my own just as a strong male leader would.

I am yet to determine how this view impacts followership and performance, but I have observed that it builds a female leader's trust, influence and authority. Nonetheless, the idea that males make better leaders than females is false and an outdated view of leadership that ignores the dynamic and complex nature of modern organizations and the evolving nature of teams.

Unfortunately, several companies maintain this misconception of leadership. It has been noted in the results of a recent study done by Amy Diehl, Leanne Dubinsky, & Amber Stephenson, (2023), posted in the Harvard Business Review, that there are instances where organizations are reluctant to hire or promote females (single or married) in their late forties because of 'much family responsibilities and impending menopause.' Women in their fifties were not hired because it is believed that 'they have 'menopause related issues and could be challenging to manage.' (Diehl, 2023 et al).

The data revealed that there is an inherent bias about female leaders. Thus, there is no right age to be a woman leader. However, there was always an age-based excuse to not take women seriously, discount their opinions, promote them or devalue their expertise and leadership skills, and declare them unfit for a leadership role.

In many instances, male leaders are hired as figureheads with misplaced authority and power, while the discounted female leader possesses the requisite expertise and skills. Unfortunately, the female leader often becomes the victim of delegation,

with her capabilities overlooked in favor of her male counterpart.

Female leaders are often held to a higher standard of accountability than their male counterparts are, and they frequently face ageism. Additionally, female leaders are more commonly marginalized due to false assumptions surrounding family responsibilities and the age-old inherent bias.

The 'Revelation' concept clearly highlights that leadership is not dependent on gender. It is important to avoid generalizing based on gender or age. Instead, we should focus on recognizing and nurturing leadership potential in all individuals. The idea that one gender is inherently better at leadership than the other is a stereotype that does not reflect the reality of leadership potential. Both men and women have the potential to be exceptional leaders.

Leadership qualities, such as empathy, communication, decisiveness, adaptability, and problem solving, are not confined to a specific gender.

Ultimately, effective leadership comes down to a combination of personal experiences, individual qualities, skills, and the ability to inspire and guide a team toward a common goal.

Leaders must be charismatic, extroverted and always positive.

The next misconception driven by leadership speculation is that leaders must be charismatic, extroverted, and always positive. Leadership is not limited to one personality type.

That said, extroverts and introverts can both be effective leaders. There is no denial that they may lead in different ways because of their different personality types, characteristics, and tendencies; nonetheless, they both can excel as leaders. They can challenge themselves in unique ways to see what they can produce.

Undoubtedly, extroversion and charisma definitely aid in leadership, as these leaders exude enthusiasm and energy; but it is certainly not the be all and end all of leadership. I strongly believe that leaders can be highly optimistic, but they can still suffer from toxic positivity.

Mark Murphy (2022) warns leaders not to confuse optimism with toxic positivity. He notes that 'rallying the team by convincing them that things are going to turn out fine is a pretty good idea. However, he explains that optimism should not just be the notion that people are going to experience positive and favorable outcomes.

Optimism includes active participation. It does not deny or ignore unpleasant realities. Optimism involves facing challenges and adversity with faith, hope, and the belief that one can overcome them.

However, problems arise when optimism turns into toxic positivity, which is an excessive and distorted form of positive thinking.

I have experienced days when I felt acute frustration because technocrats always put a positive spin on every situation, no matter how dire or tragic it may be. At one of the most stressful periods in my leadership, I was asked not to acknowledge my negative feelings and often met with dismissive responses at every level.

There were other instances where uncomfortable conversations are silenced with phrases like, 'let's not focus on the negative,' or 'I am only focusing on solutions.' I often wonder, if a leader refuses to examine and understand the challenges, concerns, and barriers surrounding an issue, how can they provide appropriate and long-lasting solutions. Negatives are a part of real life and every organization. Identifying, confronting, carefully and objectively analyzing them is the first, middle and ending steps towards lasting solutions. Any intervention program, action plan, or innovation that does not pay attention to weaknesses, mistakes or failures, is like an addict who will do anything to get his fix.

Leadership revelation confirms that when as leaders, we deny or refuse to acknowledge challenges or problems, that is not effective leadership, it is more blind management. We often fail to resolve the issues because we either dismiss them or tend to ignore them with the hope that they will magically disappear overtime. Team members who are uncertain, stressed, or overwhelmed do not feel better because you refuse to confront or remove their stressors, while telling them that they will be fine.

The key is to truthfully, practically, and realistically confront the issues, explore options and solutions, and commit to action. Truth be told, effective leaders exhibit a mix of introverted and

extroverted qualities, depending on the contexts, needs, and challenges of their team and organization.

Leaders must always be busy

The fifth misconception driven by leadership speculation is that leaders must always be busy to be productive. Leaders are sublimely encouraged to wear busyness as a badge of honor, equated with productivity and success.

Busyness has become a pervasive issue. The advancements of technology and globalization has increased the pace of work. Leaders are schooled to believe that overworking is normal, we must always be busy to succeed, busyness is equal to productivity and more worth, and that it is somehow associated with importance, opportunities, and new experiences.

Leading revelation confirms that many leaders miss lunch; have difficulty spending quality time with their family, and even miss their doctor's appointments to meet unrealistic deadlines.

In my context as a leader, I am often being asked to do more with less, and symbolically make blood out of stone. I am running from one place to the next, one meeting to another (face to face or online) or moving from one task to the other without a break. Frequently, I find myself too occupied to indulge in personal passions or execute leadership duties in the ideal manner due to the fast-paced digital environment and faulty connections that the overarching organization communication and operational structures dictate. These structures that are craftily designed to divide and conquer, as you receive numerous requests from Peter that already came from Paul with their own deadlines.

For these reasons and more, I rarely get everything done on my daily to-do list, and I am sure I am not alone

This focus on busyness can lead to a leadership style that a leader may not be proud of. It becomes so data-driven that despite having an open-door policy, the leader can find him/herself barely able to establish meaningful connections with stakeholders and team members.

In reality, there is very little reward in being busy. If you are constantly busy and not getting anything done, there is definitely something wrong. You have to break out of the established mold. You have to reframe your mindset, leadership schedule, action plan, and purposefully manage your time and prioritize tasks. You must also learn how to delegate effectively and lead with self-care.

Leading with self-care means emphasizing your own well-being, whilst still fulfilling your leadership responsibilities. Scheduling your self- care is as important as scheduling work tasks and meetings. You cannot give what you do not have. God wants us to prosper while being in good health.

It is important to prioritize your health by scheduling regular check-ups. Remember, your job may not always prioritize you, and if something happens on the job, you can be quickly replaced. Do not get so caught up in making a living that you forget to make a life for yourself.

Never substitute your family and loved ones for a job. They must always be your first priority and not an option.

Many leaders sadly realize, often too late, that while they were consumed by their job, they had unintentionally neglected their family. It is important to find a balance and not let work consume your life to the point where you miss precious moments with loved ones.

You must ensure to rest well. This also means screening your calls, turning off your phone timely, and reducing your screen time.

Leadership Is All About the Results

Another misconception by leadership speculation is that leadership is all about results. In fact, Daniel Coleman (2000) states that 'a leader's singular job is to get results. This definition of leadership constantly generates overload and cause fragmentation.

Our modern working environment is fast-paced, and sometimes, in the midst of our busy lives, we lose sight of the reasons we work; what we are truly working for; what truly matters and what is important in the now. It is important to pause and reflect on our priorities to ensure we are not just caught up in the hustle and bustle of the moment.

As humans, our life paths are not set in stone along a linear trajectory. Life's dynamics, unforeseen circumstances, and their consequences can significantly influence the outcomes we experience. Our journey is often shaped by these ever-changing factors.

In my leadership experience, I must admit that I have always anticipated positive outcomes from my deliberate and purposeful efforts, and thankfully, I have often achieved those victories, both big and small, which I have celebrated.

However, I have experienced the other side too, where my stakeholders and the technocrats in my industry wanted results every day. This forced me to focus on the drill down into getting better results, which I later learned can fester into frustration and heightened anger out of helplessness.

During my leadership journey, I have also seen a culture of data-driven or results oriented leadership taking root in numerous industries, depending on the leader, goal, vision and mission. In the education industry, which I served, there is no absence of innovations and pilot programs. Schools have become hard pressed with what Fullan (2001) refer to as too many 'disconnected, episodic, superficially adorned' and underfunded mission or projects.

He points out that in this age of uncertainty, many industries, and especially those in the midst of rapid change, are facing the added challenge of dealing with a deluge of uninvited and poorly coordinated policies and innovations from top-down bureaucratic structures.

Leadership is highly dependent on people, and leadership revelation confirms that getting results is not the primary reason why people do what they do. They work hard for the money and to improve their standard of living. If they perceive that they are not treated right, they become disengaged. Consequently, we do not always get the results we want despite exceptional efforts and hard work.

The false sentiment that results is the inevitable end product of efforts, just adds fuel to the fire of the endless cycle of initiatives that sap the strength and spirit of team members and organizations.

Research has shown that in many industries 'employee engagement is pathetically low and a great deal of this is due to the fact that organizations have lost sight of the power of leadership to connect people to the purpose of work' Forbes (2020).

Most organizations are managing their people to death by focusing only on results, but according to Fullan (2001), the process and behavior that drive authentic strategic changes aren't like
that.'

Leadership revelation forces me to agree. The misconception that leadership is about results constantly entertain the idea of poor performance. It gets even worse when the technocrats ignore their part in poor performance. Online or hybrid seminars and one-day workshops where so-called 'experts' do most of the talking without allowing much time for appreciative inquiry, focused instruction, or meaningful Q&A sessions often fall short of providing genuine training. They may share PowerPoint presentations and raise awareness but often lack the depth required for effective learning.

Poor performance commands attention, focus, careful study, contextual inquiry, and care.

I know that the view that leadership is about results can place a thorn in the side of a team leader, middle manager, and instructional leader, especially when you inherit misfits or team members who are not right for the job or who may be languishing for want of training.

At this stage, the demand for results can cause severe disengagement and foster acute disgruntlement despite good intentions.

Leadership that is about results can also make it hard for team members. When mistakes occur, and team members know that they fall short, it can make them feel vulnerable, defensive, undervalued, and unsafe.

Team members do not respond favorably, improve, or yield results when they feel on the edge. They are not lifted, motivated, or enthusiastic when they are led to fear consequences, endure negative criticism, and blame. Somali DaSilva (2022) notes that there is the double stabbing that can come from trying to 'fix people while anxiously chasing after results.

Constructive criticism can sometimes make them feel attacked rather than supported. I strongly believe that results-driven leadership does not promote diversity and inclusivity.

Rather it turns team members into competitors instead of collaborators, nailing down the disconnect, and disengagement that currently plagues many industries.

There is nothing wrong with getting results. In fact, the very best organizations generate remarkable results year after year. A great leader is also a great manager, and a great manager helps their team generate results by holding them accountable in a dignified and supportive way.

Leadership revelation has taught me that team members can only improve through coaching, better direction and second chances, which requires quality time that is a scarce commodity in results driven leadership. The fact is a 'leader's job is to connect the purpose of everyone on their team with the purpose of the organization, so they are intrinsically motivated and excited about their work'.

Failure is not an option in successful leadership

Finally, there is also a misconception that failure is not an option in successful leadership. This could not be further from the truth. Leadership is a tough job and can be a marathon of trial and error. Nothing about leadership is foolproof or cast in stone.

Failure must be seen as a friend with a split personality. It can drive fear into a leader or make them point the finger or find someone or something to blame. Alternatively, it can be viewed as a schoolmaster for effective and authentic leadership that adds clarity and purpose and carry significance rather than success.

In my experience as a leader and in my context, whenever there is a crisis or a problem, leaders are usually expected to jump into action for quick results to appease the hierarchical bureaucracies. The technocrats want to keep things moving and they are rarely curious, but very anxious or toxic when they stop. Taking a step back gives them the unwanted signal that you are failing and that you will have very little success. They may hasten to adopt and implement best practices from other schools as a quick fix.

Leadership revelation has taught me that a best practice that works well with one set of team members and yields excellent results can become a worst practice when applied to another group. Innovation and creativity require an environment where people feel comfortable making mistakes, being vulnerable, and knowing that their contributions are valued.

This fosters a culture of growth and innovation.

Significance cannot be measured with the benchmark we use for success. In today's society, success usually acquires value based on who or what it is compared with, and whose hand it is in. Two people can acquire the same thing and one is described as highly successful and the other lucky.

Significance on the other hand is felt and experienced by others and carries unprecedented value as its effect is shared or distributed. Leaders must embrace mistakes or failure as a gateway to building a solution- oriented culture with their team, a community of practice, and a quality education circle; a repertoire of best practices of their exploration and road to growth and improvement.

This is a meaningful and purposeful way of celebrating the wins and the journey it took to get there. By failing, leaders can learn from their mistakes and grow to become effective critical thinkers and problem solvers. The willingness to do so also sets an example for the rest of the organization that it is ok to make mistakes, learn from them, and get better as a result.

Great leaders embrace failure in life and see it as a great tool or one of the best ways to investigate improvement.

The Bottom Line

In summing up this chapter, you may be wondering as a Christian leader in your professional space what should be your response to these misconceptions.

I would say, as Christian leaders we are to focus on being relevant in your professional space. By virtue of your position, core values and faith, you are held to a higher level of accountability in all aspects of your service. How you present yourself to God, and how you lead are at the heart of your service.

You should view and respond to leadership misconceptions with patience, understanding, and a commitment to truth and education. This means, that as leaders, you must have exceptional clarity about who you are, and who you are not. You must establish your own code of conduct as you cannot just go with the flow. Outdated misconceptions of leadership need to be put aside and replaced with the correct ones.

It is essential for you to understand your inner values and beliefs, as they guide you in discerning what is ethically and morally incorrect. In every field, industry, or organization that you serve, you need to develop your own code of ethics. Your ethics govern your principles; how you come across to your team members and stakeholders and how you give away your power to others. To convincingly defy the myths of leadership you must lead with a resounding example. When you demonstrate the correct concepts of leadership and team leaders and stakeholders see you embodying the values you promote, it can challenge misconceptions and inspire positive change.

You are anointed, appointed, and purposefully commissioned to lead with kindness. Leading with kindness does not mean that you are always agreeable, neither does this mean that you are disagreeable or points to aggressiveness. It means that you have a balanced integration of emotion and logic.

You 'can be angry and sin not'-(Eph. 4:26). You must intentionally use an approach that ensures you are responding rather than reacting. It is not about being nice with patience or compromising to avoid confrontations, mitigate problems or keep the peace. It involves approaching these confrontations assertively, skillfully finding common ground, and establishing rapport while calmly engaging in those challenging conversations. Your feedback must also make people feel supported and not attacked.

It means you understand and make sense of what is going on in your organization and industry and effect any change that is needed.

It means that you understand the power of connections and collaborations to drive the organization's vision, mission, and policies. It means you know and understand that you control situations and not people.

It means that you must be adaptable, resilient, and prepared for the new threats present in a rapidly changing workplace, knowledge sharing, workplace demographics, and disruptive technology.

It means you hold yourself accountable by taking responsibility for your actions, and by generating a positive view of the future that others take on as their own.

It means that you understand and accept your God-given assignment, and who is in ultimate control.

It means assisting individuals in becoming masters of their destiny, managing their emotions, and recognizing their control over their lives and ability to learn from mistakes. It also entails forming partnerships, posing the right questions, receiving appropriate answers, and inspiring your team to adopt a solution- oriented approach that benefits your organization. Encouraging your team to challenge themselves, collaborate, and learn alongside others at all levels is another important aspect of it.

The truth is, leadership is a multifaceted and evolving concept with various challenges and intricacies. Your goal is not to prove others wrong, but to guide them towards a more accurate and enriching understanding of leadership and representation of Christian leadership in a professional space

. As you reflect on the concepts presented in this chapter, ask yourself these questions;

What are the leadership misconceptions that has influenced my leadership style?

What are my current leadership pain points, and how can I overcome them in order not to convey a false image of success?

Leadership Nugget

'Leadership is neither showmanship nor dictatorship. Leadership is a stewardship and a partnership' – Rick Warren

Let us pray:,

Dear God,

Help me bring a clear and true understanding of leadership under the submission of the light of Christ and give me the clarity I need to lead victoriously and authentically. Amen.

Chapter 9

Navigating Through Leadership Pain and Uncertainty

'-For we are God's workmanship, created in Christ's Jesus to do good works, which God prepared in advance for us to do 'Ephesian 2:10.

Sam Chand makes a brilliant observation that got me thinking about leadership pains and uncertainty. He explains that 'when leaders in any field take the risk of moving individuals and organizations from one stage to another, from stagnation to effectiveness, or from success to significance, they inevitably encounter confusion, passivity, and outright resistance from those they're trying to lead.' I could not agree more.

He also explains that 'all leadership is a magnet for pain,' which comes in many forms. We face great pressure and sometimes oppression for bad decisions or mistakes, and harsh criticism for our good decisions because 'we've changed the beloved status quo.' However, he points out that pain is not the enemy; rather it is the inability or unwillingness to face pain that is a far greater danger.

He advocates that Christian leaders in a professional space have a greater difficulty handling leadership pain and uncertainty, than secular leaders. This is because Christian leaders tend to look on God promises and conclude that by virtue of their stewardship and profession of faith, God must attend them with joy, support, favor, and success.

A popular preacher once said that if you are a Christian leader, influencer, educator, employer, or employee, service is not optional. You are born in a community and for the community.

You are intentionally designed and fashioned to serve him. Your personality traits are not accidental. Your abilities, gifts, interests, talents, expertise, and life experiences are not haphazardly allocated. You are created with a special area of expertise, unique gifts, and talents. You are given your unique assignment to prepare you for your God given ministry whether it be carpentry, music, arts or leadership.

In previous chapters, we learned how God lovingly shapes you for your ministry.

Repeatedly, he fashions your clay into form until you become a vessel of honor pruned for purpose. We have discovered that one of the critical ways to gain this understanding is through a wilderness experience or a leadership crisis. Additionally, we have come to realize that significance is often more valuable than mere success, as it provides life and mission with meaning, relevance, and purpose.

I believe you understand and amplify your mission when you grow from your leadership pain and navigate through leadership adversity.

Leadership pains take many forms, but they do not occur until you become a leader. These challenges can range from life-threatening situations to more common experiences like self- doubt, fear of losing control, insecurity, and feelings of helplessness. They often stem from a struggle to accept both the limitations and possibilities inherent in leadership.

One important principle of leadership is that no one becomes an effective leader without experiencing or knowing pain. As mentioned in previous chapters, pain can cause you to either retreat or keep going. One thing is certain, both bring their own share of hurt, regret, or growth.

In this chapter, I aim to bring attention to the often-overlooked and inevitable challenges of leadership, which transcend the superficial aspects of popularity contests, subscribers, and likes. It is where the rubber hits the road. It is where courage, faith, and patience are needed to face down the dark side of leadership. You have to confront the sides of leadership you wish would just disappear.

This is certainly not an easy task. It can be excruciating, and often heartbreaking. However, what I know from my own experience is that these leadership pains allow you to get to know yourself better, and what you are made of. It prompts you to approach and treat yourself with compassion, value your individuality and authenticity, and summon motivation and fortitude from deep within to confront those unwanted or difficult feelings that always accompany pain.

The Pain of Being Misunderstood

Effective and authentic servant leaders are frequently subject to misunderstanding, even when they take every conceivable measure to prevent it. They may pray earnestly for guidance, invest significant effort in their work, and communicate their plans impeccably, yet still find themselves facing misconceptions.

This does not include the instances when there is a lack of clarity in communication. Rather, it refers to a time when others judge you or your character, based on misinformation they have received.

As a leader, experiencing frequent misunderstandings can be a lonely, challenging, and draining ordeal. It can be disheartening to engage with others when it seems like your words and actions are consistently misinterpreted and underappreciated.

Additionally, stakeholders and team members may ignore how you are feeling, or do not care how you are feeling and can become indifferent or accuse you of being unlovable in some way. This can lead to leadership and stakeholders' misunderstandings and conflict. It can also result in false assumptions that can portray you in the worst possible light. This can hurt a leader deeply. No one likes to be labelled, criticized, judged, or misunderstood.

As a Christian leader in your professional space, you have to learn how to personally and professionally, grow through your pain and dubiety because your ultimate responsibility and divine command is not to react but respond, by modelling the behavior you would like to see in others. You are admonished to be kind, tenderhearted, and forgiving one another in love (Eph. 4:32); although an attack on your character may put you in defense mode, and you may be tempted to use your authority and power to discipline the offenders.

It is best to practice the discipline of humility. Ground yourself in your divine appointment, assignment, purpose, and mission. Reflect deeply to see what truth may be in the midst of falsehoods, what path may be used for reconciliation, and what direction you need to follow. Tony Baron (2020), suggests that another way to deal with the pain of being misunderstood is to practice the discipline of civility.

Pause to reflect before you engage people and recognize the pain or anxiety behind their words. He states that to grow from the pain of being misunderstood, while 'claiming and caring for one's identity, needs and beliefs it must be done without degrading someone else' in the process.

The Pain of Unexpected Resignations

It is a valid perspective that people often leave an organization when they feel disgruntled, overlooked, or undervalued. However, it is essential to recognize that some staff members depart as part of a healthy and normal staff transition. This can include:

a. Moving nearer to home and family
b. Relocating with family because of the upward movement of one partner
c. Completion of tenure
d. Poor performance
e. Illness
f. No opportunity for upward mobility
g. Their support partners have moved on
h. Migrate to another city or country
i. Exit into their own business

The other side of this coin is that sometimes the people that you help the most are the ones that complain the most or leave your organization without honor. You chose them, hired them, paid them, encouraged them, loved them, trained them, and they become difficult and sometimes hurtful.

I have had my fair share of employees leaving my institution unexpectedly because of their own doing, professional misconduct, or because they have personal relational issues with supervisors and middle managers.

In my organization, I also have instances where one partner resigned, and the other partner took early retirement to support his partner on the new career path.

I have had an instance when one staff member

took early retirement to cash in on an extremely appealing pension or retirement package and took three other staff members with him that were in the same age group and with common interests and community ties.

There was also another occasion when three of my best and brightest team members resigned because of a staff member who constantly got upset and often antisocial when she did not get her way or become offended when her opinion was not lauded, elevated, or sufficiently recognized.

When this gets out of hand, leaders have to make the painful and difficult choice to prepare an exit notice. In my context, this individual chose to resign instead of being fired to not hurt her chances for a new employment.

Despite this, I paid a high and painful price because three of my excellent team players had unexpectedly resigned and had already gone through the gate. Regardless of the reasons, it is painful when staff members leave, especially when they take other staff members with them.

I have learned that when good employees leave, it causes a painful displacement and can have a negative jerk reaction. Panache (2019) and other experts confirm this by stating that 'when multiple people leave an organization, it creates a chain reaction among colleagues.'
One researcher stated that, 'when one good employee leaves, it signals to others that it might be time to take stock of their options, what researchers call, 'turnover contagion.' This departure can produce

shock waves, especially for a leader who begins to wonder if there is something that he/she had missed.

Growing through this leadership pain requires Christian leaders to exercise patience and maintain respectful communication, even in the face of slights and hurts. This is the most challenging aspect of the process, as it demands professionalism and impartiality simultaneously.

Christian leaders have a responsibility to encourage departing staff members to engage in self-reflection, assessing their strengths, weaknesses, and areas for character development. They should approach this process with love and seek peaceful interactions, offering guidance and support to help these individuals grow and mature.

The pain of deep disappointment and loss

Effective leaders often encounter situations where plans do not go as expected, people may not be who they seem, performance issues arise from seemingly capable team members, or disappointing results follow diligent effort. It is an inherent part of leadership to address these challenges.

The loss of loved ones and support partners can also serve a devastation blow. These are moments when effective leaders experience disappointment and frustration. Disappointment and loss tend to have adverse effects on a leader personally and professionally. In these painful moments, leaders can feel sad, angry, ashamed, and demotivated, simply because in these moments you realize and have to accept that even when you think you are superhuman, you are just human.

Leaders often spend a significant portion of their lives at work, and their sense of purpose, meaning, and even personal and professional dramas can become closely tied to their workplace experiences.

As a leader, you cannot ignore the emotions that come with deep disappointment and loss.

Colleagues, mentors, and counselors with good intentions may encourage you to tone down or try to ignore the emotions and move ahead with the challenge in front of you.

I have learned that as a leader, when you fail to address your disappointments and frustrations, you nourish your mind, body, and soul with the building blocks of a crisis or meltdown. You dishonor yourself and those dependent on you. I have learned the hard way the importance of dealing with those emotions that come from a deep disappointment or loss.

My leadership journey has been riddled with loss and disappointment, or joys and sorrows. I can vividly remember when my father, who was my greatest real male model and most trustworthy advisor, unexpectedly passed away. To date, the pain is indescribable. It was such a deep loss on several levels. Every single day, I literally had to put my best foot forward and pray without ceasing to get through my workday.

I was unable to talk about this loss or come to grips with it for a very long time.

Sundays, which were meant for spending quality time together, became the worst days for me in terms of pain. There were many Sundays when I couldn't even get out of bed, struggled to explain what I was going through to others, and found it challenging to coach myself into recovery, despite being a coach myself.

I often felt like an imposter when people in both my personal and professional life faced similar losses and turned to me for coaching or support. It was surprising to me that in assisting them in their recovery, I found my own path to healing.

In hindsight, I realized that this was God's way of helping me grow through my pain.

Exactly one year after, in the heart of my overcoming process, my spiritual father, mentor, and divine destiny helper, passed away. I was devastated. He held not just a special place in my heart but also served as my motivation for staying in my organization. Furthermore, he was the heart of our community. You see, as a leader, I firmly believe that every community possesses both a heart and a brain.

The 'heart' and 'brain' of every community metaphorically represent the emotional and intellectual centers that drive and sustain how a community function. The 'heart of a community typically represents the people who contribute to and promote the emotional wellbeing, social cohesion, and sense of belonging in a community.

The 'heart' of the community not only influences by leading it towards good and right actions, but also represents the collective emotions, values, and connections that bind individuals together. His death not only sent shock waves throughout the professional community, but it also ignited community grief and anguish.

The "brain" of the community symbolizes the organizational and intellectual core, comprising individuals who influence decision-making, planning, problem-solving, and play a pivotal role in shaping the community's development.

The brain is responsible for guiding the community's future, ensuring that it adapts to change and address challenges in a systematic manner. It is a concept that I have developed in another book.

As a leader, I became a part of the community to mourn the loss of a mentor who had become more like a father and prayer partner to me.

A man who played a vital role in fostering and maintaining a positive atmosphere, building positive relationships, and providing support to everyone in times of need.

A man who nurtured the social fabric of the community and ensured that it remained a welcoming and supportive place for all its members. I still grieve for this precious soul, but I find solace in growing through this leadership pain by becoming part of a foundation that symbolizes his legacy of care, support, and love.

The most earth-shattering loss I have experienced to date is the passing of my mother. It still feels like yesterday. This loss disrupted every area of my life. I just could not function. I was numb for weeks. The pain was and still is so deep and far reaching that I still cannot talk about its devastating effects on me, and how it has impacted my professional journey, so I wrote several poems. I share the first poem I wrote a few days after I kept calling her phone and didn't get the desired answer.

The pain of death is black. Indescribable, despairing, gruesome, real black.

Packed with ifs…should haves…. could haves….

Horribly, unfathomably dull. DEATH

Sees you, seeks you, haunts you, pursues you, captures you.

Begins your judgement…HOPE –the blessed hope. The only ointment.

I learned that for a leader to grow through the pain of loss, you have to be open, and trust yourself enough to confront your loss in a timely manner. You have to be vulnerable, patient, and honest with yourself.

You must have a support group and a profound, intimate relationship with God, believing that He knows what is best and that everything will ultimately work out for your good. Ask questions that keep you grounded in the present while preparing for the future. Engage in activities that align with your core values and mission.

Allow their legacy to live on through you.

Amidst all of this, I struggled with the profound disappointment of realizing that two individuals I had hired and brought onto my staff turned out to be different from who they had initially presented themselves to be.

I had the unfortunate experience of hiring these new members of staff, whose influence proved detrimental to the organization. They came highly recommended and were equally impressive in the interview. They were quite likeable at first, as they appeared very nice and helpful. However, one turned out to be a silent critic (passive-aggressive) and the other was directly aggressive (narcissistic).

Let me pause here to briefly highlight the subtle and destructive impact of the silent critic.

The silent critic is highly amicable, works very close with the leader, and appears to be loyal but is unknowingly disgruntled. The silent critic raises issues and agrees with the leader in private but offers no public voice for team members to hear constructive criticism. They have a remarkable influence behind the scenes and speak with a crafty voice of division that cause unsuspecting team members to doubt the sincerity of the leader.

The silent critic thrives in the shadows, meticulously avoids the light, causing people to be angry with the leader, and often uses slander to diminish trust for leadership. They always appear supportive, reasonable, and understanding of the leader, but conceals hatred with lying lips. They purposefully and intentionally spread division, and is never silent, but you hardly hear them speak in public. They are nothing but backstabbers.

Four months after joining the staff, they had garnered a significant following, with team members eagerly listening to their words and taking cues from them during meetings. A few staff members emulated the code of dress of one directly aggressive employee. Most of their colleagues admired them because they displayed exceptional talents in art, design, and music.

Their inflated sense of self and irrational desire to always be the center of attention, while pretending to be introverts, caused them to appear impressive, inflated their influence, and generated colleague or peer loyalty.

Getting these individuals to meet deadlines and grasp the challenges of leadership became an ongoing struggle for leaders at every level within my organization. This contributed to dissatisfaction among staff members and created a rift between leaders and key team members.

These individuals did not respond positively to constructive feedback; they often felt attacked rather than supported, regardless of how accommodating others tried to be. One of them, in particular was very calculating and tended to complain about everything.

First, it was her supervisors, then her colleagues that were not a part of her fan club. More significantly, she had no solution for every problem she created and blamed everyone for her mistakes. She could not be an amicable team player unless she was the one leading the group. After being there for one year, they completely divided the staff.

They skillfully created mistrust among long-standing staff members and fully expected to get special treatment from everyone around them.

Those members of staff, who did not comply with making them the center of attention, innocently became their sworn enemies.

The most aggressive of the two would often be heard telling long-winded stories about her life, family, brilliance, achievements, and success that was not translated into her professional performance, which was so disappointing. She would display an envious spirit if any member of staff got recognition and would subtly undermine and discredit them.

Eventually, she was called out by her own actions and resigned her post, taking one long- standing team member with her. The dishonorable way in which she left was what was most painful and disappointing, especially since innocent loyalists chose to go with her.

Nonetheless, many staff members openly expressed relief, but sadly, a residue of her defiant spirit was left behind. Additionally, her remaining fan club members on staff began to weigh their options because of her mindset disruption, and correspondingly it took some time for them to settle back in as productive team players. Several months later, the silent critic also resigned in a dishonorable way that left so much sadness and anger behind.

Conversely, at the start of your leadership journey, you may experience failure and your organization's failure can become a disappointing reoccurrence that can leave you hanging with a range of emotions. The oppressive expectations and impatience of key stakeholders can drive a painful nail into this coffin.

As a leader, you may find yourself overcommitting, skipping meals, neglecting quality time with your family, and repeatedly missing doctor's appointments in an effort to improve overall performance. However, despite your best efforts, you may not achieve the desired results. This can lead to self-blame, a tendency to blame others, anxiety, fear, sadness, guilt, and a sense of isolation.

As a leader, you're not only tasked with improving results, but you also have to find a way to motivate and engage disengaged team members who have consistently avoided achieving desired outcomes. This often requires you to go beyond the call of duty, sacrificing personal time, and dealing with team members who are despondent and discouraged due to persistent poor performance. The disappointment and pain you feel can lead to an acute and increasing fear of failure, and burnout, which is not an easy challenge to overcome. You may even contemplate whether it is time to move on or quit.

I have to highlight that disappointment is a formidable adversary for Christian leaders in the workplace. Therefore, as a leader, it is essential to allow yourself to feel the disappointment.

Heather Whalley (2019) says, 'if you are hit with a crushing disappointment at work, you must give yourself permission to stop and feel, and name what you are feeling'. You must also release the emotion through crying, writing, dancing, running, or whatever works for you to release.'

She highlights that many leaders 'do not allow themselves to acknowledge the sadness or anger caused by the disappointment. As a result, the emotions get struck ruminating around in our head and body.'

When you choose to dismiss, suppress, or package your emotions, or when others encourage you to do so, you are doing yourself a disservice. These unresolved emotions tend to resurface later on. By acknowledging and assessing your disappointment, you do not allow the pain to paralyze you, persuade you to quit, or refuse to face a challenging situation without an effort, or without a fight. That said, the fight is not the main issue. The main issue is the 'reason' we are fighting. Christian leaders have to be resilient, lead faithfully, and utilize their God-given discernment.

The pain when leadership decisions bring pain to others

A wise man said that effective leaders ignite real change. The process involves doing what is usually painful. It causes organizational upheaval and personal torment, as very often the decisions that leaders have to make inflict pain on team members. This can be extremely painful for a leader. Generally, good leaders or Christians in leadership are not people who get pleasure from the pain of others; neither do they enjoy hurting others. They are just responsible for making difficult decisions in the short-term for the long-term benefit of advancing the particular mission of the organization they lead.

An example of this is the inability to extend the contract of a temporary or provisionally appointed employee, even though they are a promising and highly dedicated worker who deserves to remain with the company. This situation arises due to the bureaucratic challenges associated with removing a permanent employee who consistently underperforms.

Another example is when you have to make the difficult decision after being forced to downsize, knowing that the individuals selected lack the financial security and opportunity for immediate employment. These decisions can produce painful consequences for everyone involved.

The pain that comes from sharing the pain of others

The final area of pain that leaders often overlook is the burden of sharing in the pains, hurts, and disappointments of their teammates or staff members. Sometimes, as leaders, we often shoulder the burden and pain of others, while neglecting our own needs.

As a leader, I have had to understand and help some teammates carry the pain of betrayal, a painful separation, and even messy divorces. All of these issues negatively affected productivity, decrease motivation, and fuel depression in a small community. The pain is also manifested in other ways, which include paranoia (caused from what was perceived as prolonged embarrassment and abuse), low self-esteem, and antisocial behavior based on the perception that they have lost value and significance in the eyes of their colleagues and stakeholders.

I shared the grief with parents and team players and their families when they suffer the loss of a child, or extended close family member, experienced a personal crisis or trauma and the pain of a colleague's miscarriage.

The truth is, leaders are not exempt from relating and connecting to the needs and struggles of team members. Nor are we exempt from understanding the emotions of others and assisting people in facing, managing, and comprehending their feelings and emotions. In fact, leaders who insist on separating these emotions from work are often seen as insensitive, cold-hearted, and lacking in empathy and compassion.

However, I have learned that 'it is not the load that breaks you down it is the way you carry it' (Lena Horne), if someone in my personal or professional space needs help, there is no harm in helping them carry their load. We just have to learn how to unload it when it starts weighing us down. When we fully immerse ourselves in the burdens and pains of our team members, so much so that we neglect our own, we make a serious mistake. Continually dwelling on other people's pain and feeling the obligation to fully experience their suffering can leave us overwhelmed and unable to function.

There are instances when it can become so heartbreaking that it begins to negatively impact our health and productivity. Sadly, this pain becomes more pronounced when you have been there for everyone else, and especially during your toughest times, no one is there for you.

Always remember, as a Christian leader, you can only carry so much and no more. Embrace the reality, set the correct boundaries and refer the people in need of help for support. Connect them with people who can provide mentorship and guidance along the way.

It is imperative to understand and accept that pain is a part of life and leadership. Navigating and growing through pain and uncertainty is not easy, but it is essential for walking a path of significance. Therefore, my advice is to welcome pain as a friend, and not an enemy.

Your pain tells you when you are moving in the right direction. According to Sam Chand (2020), 'new pains will always be a part of your life as you continue climbing the ladder to your destiny'. Never let your discomfort or heartache be wasted. Ask the right questions and learn the lessons from your pain. Use it to change, stretch, adapt, and press into your calling, assignment, and purpose. As you reflect on the concepts in this chapter, ask yourself these questions:

As a Christian leader, how do I handle my leadership challenges?

How do I cope with loss, disappointment, misunderstandings, and unexpected resignations?

Am I taking on too much of another people's pain?

As a Christian leader, what are my pain points?

Leadership Nugget

'There is no growth without change, no change without loss, and no loss without pain' – (Samuel R. Chand).

Let us pray:

Dear Lord,

Be near me in my time of weakness and pain. Reveal my character flaws to me and help me repair them. Place in me the navigational ability so that I can grow from my leadership pain. Please give me your perspective to fulfil your vision as a leader. Amen

Chapter 10

The Christian Leader's Pain Points

- "I can do nothing on my own initiative. As I hear, I judge; and my judgment is just, because I do not seek my own will, but the will of Him who sent me." John 5:30

In a professional space, Christian leaders may encounter several pain points. How we endure and overcome them is the crucial opening for how God works grace deeply into our lives. Ellen White (1927) explains that Christian leaders can become men of responsibility and influence if they unite the power of their will with divine strength and earnestly engage in their work.

As was highlighted in previous chapters, Christian leaders are anointed, appointed, and commissioned to fulfil a higher calling, higher character and greater accountability in service to self, humankind, and God.

A higher calling is not something we receive through training and education. Rather, it is a direct appointment from God. Therefore, to respond to a higher calling means that we must do the will of God joyfully, conscientiously, and dutifully, knowing that God gives the ultimate reward to every man.

A higher character means living a life that is approved by God. Ellen White embodies a wholesome definition of Christian character that states that 'strength of character consists of two things: the power of will and the power of self- control'. She highlights that the real greatness and nobility of the man is measured by the power of the feelings that he subdues and not the power of the feelings that subdue him. The strongest man is he who, while sensitive to abuse, will yet restrain passion and forgive his enemies. Such men are true heroes.

A greater level of accountability means doing what you have been assigned to do well and having the confidence to know what you can do by yourself, and what you can only do with God's help. It means utilizing our appointment, abilities, talents, skills, professional relationships, and opportunities in a God- honoring way. It places on us a greater responsibility to exercise our mental powers and avoid intellectual slothfulness. It involves regular self-reflection and intense study, which expand strengthen, and develop the mind.

This means that a Christian leader's pain points are always rooted in testing of your faith, morality, core values, and doing what is right and just. However, these pain points may vary depending on the specific industry, organizational culture, and individual circumstances of Christian leaders in the professional space.

One challenging pain point of a Christian leader is balancing faith and work. Christian leaders may struggle with finding a balance between their faith and the demands of their professional roles. Following Christ's teachings in the workplace can be very hard, especially when you are being misunderstood, judged, critiqued, and maligned for doing the right thing and putting the needs of others before your own.

Sometimes, even prioritizing the needs of others above your own, results in conflicts. The pressure of remaining a Christian role model and applying the teachings of Christ to be tender hearted certainly intensifies in these instances.

A fierce battle often arises between your humanity and your Christian values when faced with unreasonable demands and hostile treatment in an unethical work environment.

Similarly, as a Christian leader, you may struggle with maintaining a work-life balance. You may constantly miss lunch, doctor's and dentist appointments, and miss spending quality time with the family and friends.

Additionally, the demands of your leadership roles, coupled with personal and family commitments, can make it challenge to allocate time for spiritual practices, church involvement, and personal growth. This can create internal conflicts or allow a leader to suffer from 'imposter syndrome'. This can also result in a greater spiritual dilemma as they struggle to align their faith to their actions.

Christian leaders often face ethical dilemmas that challenge their core values and principles. These dilemmas may involve conflicts of interest, integrity maintenance, or addressing moral concerns within the organization, including issues related to behavior, work performance, and organizational culture.

You may face pressure to compromise your beliefs or engage in practices that conflict with your moral convictions. For example, you may be requested to adjust the casual leave days of a coworker, who has exhausted the required days, to a sick leave facility, although he or she is not sick.

In another instance, you may be asked to approve a coworker's sick leave, who's clearly not sick and is seen in excellent health shopping at a mall. You may also be asked by superiors to avoid telling stakeholders the truth, give employees half-truths, or embellish a particular situation to get a desired outcome. You may face pressure to compromise your integrity or engage in unethical practices to fit into a prescribed mode of leadership and achieve professional success.

Christian leaders can also experience workplace discrimination or bias because of your faith. You may face challenges, such as exclusion from certain decisions, functions, or even a well-deserved promotion. You may be ridiculed or oppressed for dressing modestly, avoiding certain conversations, and for doing and standing up for what is right, rather than what is popular.

You can also be a victim of unfair treatment or limitations on expressing your religious beliefs when necessary, and the reasons for your actions or decisions. This can become quite problematic in a diverse professional environment, as having to navigate interactions with individuals who hold differing beliefs or conflicting values can contribute to or create a hostile work environment.

This can lead to challenges in decision-making, teamwork, and building healthy relationships. Therefore, as a Christian leader, you may need to navigate issues related to diversity and inclusion in the workplace. You are also responsible for fostering an inclusive environment that respects the beliefs and values of individuals from various backgrounds.

The final pain point that I will address in this chapter is the heightened scrutiny and criticism that Christian leaders face. You cannot win the battle with the seasoned naysayers, who have extra expectations and scrutinize your every move due to your faith-based leadership role.

You have very little wriggle room. If you, at any time lose an iota of self-control and self- discipline under intense pressure, you lose your followers' trust. This can be emotionally and mentally challenging and require you to navigate accountability with grace and humility.

Balancing assertiveness, accountability, Christian values, and humility can indeed be a delicate task for Christian leaders in a professional space. Staying true to your values and maintaining personal integrity can present significant challenges in the face of conflicting demands and ethical dilemmas.

To conclude, I have learned that to cope with these pain points, a Christian leader must remain vigilant and proactive in identifying and addressing potential issues. Monitor the climate, so you can be prepared to adapt to changing circumstances. Cultivate a culture of continuous improvement and proactive leadership.

Encourage open feedback, innovation, and a willingness to learn from mistakes. Emphasize the importance of ethical behavior and responsible Christian leadership.

As you reflect on this chapter, ask yourself these questions:

Which pain point have I encountered as a Christian leader?

Have I remained true to my core values and beliefs?

How am I reflecting my calling and character and holding myself personally accountable?

What are the mistakes that I must avoid?

Leadership Nugget

When the whole world is silent, even one voice becomes powerful." —Malala Yousafzai, activist.

Let us pray:

Dear God,

Help me remain true to my calling, and reflect your character amidst discrimination, alienation, ethical dilemmas, criticism, and pain. Help me do things that I can do and leave those things that only you can do. Amen.

Chapter 11

Leadership Mistakes to Avoid

"For we all stumble in many ways. And if anyone does not stumble in what she says, he is a perfect man able to bridle his whole body" (James 3:2).

Leadership is undoubtedly an ongoing, learning, evolving and ever-growing process. John Maxwell suggests that this is so because leaders go through five levels of leadership.

Level one points to the position level, where individuals follow the leader primarily because they are obligated to or solely because it is the means through which they receive their paycheck. Interestedly, at this level, the team members only invest the least amount of their energy, effort, time and ability.

Level two refers to the permission level, where people follow you because they want to. At this stage, you start to cultivate and exhibit a servant leadership mindset. This involves acquiring essential relationship skills by actively observing and listening to the needs of your followers.

Next comes the third level, which is described as the production level. At this stage, people follow you because of what you have. You lead by example, and people follow you for your efficiency, productivity, and problem-solving attitude.

Your growth, actions, and responses to your followers' needs takes you to the fourth level, where people follow you because of what you have done and continue to do for them. Your primary focus at this level is to develop people.

Your leadership development, progression, and influence climaxes at level five, called the pinnacle level. At this level, a leader gains significance, which is the unbridled respect of followers.

During this stage, everyone may not necessarily like the leader, but you are undeniably respected. This respect stems from your willingness to make tough decisions that may not be popular but are in the best interest of both the people and the organization.

It takes time and effort for a leader to get to level five, but in the end, it is worth it. Of course, being a leader is no easy feat. It is never an easy transition. Every leader messes up and make mistakes during their journey

After serving as a leader for more than a decade, I have shaped my own definition of leadership, overcame numerous leadership crisis, moved through the five levels of leadership, and completed different levels of leadership assignments.

I have come to realize that some of the best lessons are learned when you reach the limits of your abilities, grapple with mistakes, encounter setbacks, and confront failure head-on. To many bureaucrats, this may be seen as a minus and not a plus. There is zero tolerance for leadership mistakes, and very little room to grow and expand through trial and error. Many who display and model this intolerance have contributed to the downfall of the bright and promising leaders and their organizations. This issue highlights a very destructive character flaw and mindset that leads to leadership canker and disease.

As Albert Einstein stated, 'who has never made a mistake has never tried anything new'. What we need to understand is that failure is not the opposite of success; it is a crucial part of it.

Success knocks at your door when you have survived all of your mistakes. Any opinion that does not consider this is based on a theoretical and speculative definition of leadership rather than a valid and authentic definition that comes through the revelation gathered via immersion and experience. Your experiences, setbacks, failures, and mistakes endorse you to be the leader you were purposefully commissioned to be.

Every profession or calling needs a mission statement, and every leader needs an assignment or involvement in something that is bigger or larger than they are. When a Christian leader understands his or her assignment, mission, appointment, or calling, and unites it with a servant leader's mindset, they define leadership in terms of service and significance.

My definition of leadership is adapted from Bill Lawrence, Bible.org. I feel that it describes my core value and expectations regarding leadership.

"Leadership is the act of influencing and serving others out of Christ's interests in their lives, so they accomplish God's purposes for and through them".

My reference point has its roots in servant leadership, which in my opinion, equals love for God that makes me a servant of God and love for my fellowman, which results in service to my fellowman. My primary focus is not rooted in worldly notions of success, such as the love of money or power. Rather it is rooted in voluntary service that carries an eternal reward.

In previous chapters, I presented a wholesome discussion on the misconceptions of leadership, leadership assignments, and leadership pain points. These notions are often misdirected, ignored, glossed over or mostly unaddressed. In this chapter, I addressed some crucial mistakes or leadership practices that must be avoided or discarded, if we are to be truly effective as Christian leaders in our professional space.

Through my experiences, both positive and negative, I have gained a valuable perspective on the often-overlooked aspects of leadership.

Frequently, individuals enthusiastically follow technocratic and bureaucratic directives issued by those in positions of authority. However, these directives may not encompass the essence of genuine leadership.

There are numerous leadership programmers, commonly called mentors, that are hired by organizations, (God knows I have had my share of them). Unfortunately, some of these programs perceive effective leadership as merely achieving compliance and getting people to do what you want, rather than focusing on inspiring and empowering individuals to discover their untapped potential and achieve feats they never thought possible.

They view transformational leadership as an unwavering commitment to persuading individuals to go where they may not want to be but should be, instead of fostering an environment that empowers and enables them to willingly pursue growth and achievement to get to where they ought to be.

What is more alarming is that they would highlight you as the epitome or excellence if you demonstrate the ability to motivate self and others enough that they go beyond the call of duty to correlate and submit data. This makes you an exceptional leadership or at least one of your industry's best.

The leadership programmer is self-motivated and motivates others to constantly ignore self- love and care and hardly get to spend quality time with their family to guarantee the success of an innovation or pilot program. These leadership programmers, posing as mentors, often forget or are too busy to call you when you get sick, burnout, or overwhelmed from overwork or inadequate self-care or personal inattentiveness.

Twenty years from now, the only people to remember that you worked late will be your family. Many ministries and many organizations are involved in the numbers and data game, but each can be destroyed because of attention to numbers rather than people. Empowering employees is the greatest revenue builder in any organization.

Leaders, who are not given the opportunity to carry the burden of helping, supporting, and empowering the vulnerable in their organization or ministry, will never achieve leadership significance.

True leadership significance arises from effectively serving others, meeting their needs, and goes beyond mere data-driven results that focus solely on individual achievement.

Jesus Himself spoke against this when expressing the importance of serving. He says, "You know that the rulers of the Gentiles lord it over them, and those who are great exercise authority over them. Yet it shall not be so among you; but whoever desires to become great among you, let him be your servant. And whoever desires to be first among you, let him be your slave — just as the Son of Man did not come to be served, but to serve, and to give His life a ransom for many." (Matt. 20: 25).

Leadership mistakes are made both subconsciously and consciously, and are often the results of 'evil programming,' which refers to our examples, experience, mentors, guide, cultural norms, speculation, and teachings about what leadership is, how it must be translated, and the manner in which it must be distributed.

The leadership mistakes highlighted in this chapter include misunderstanding of leadership, leadership roles, training, motivation, feedback, delegation, succession planning and resilience.

Misunderstanding Leadership

One of the many mistakes that we have been programmed by the system to make is misunderstanding of leadership. The leadership framework advocated by a vast number of leadership frameworks and prototypes is the top-down leadership. This approach is widespread in my industry despite pious pronouncements regarding the importance of consensus and transformational leadership. It represents a method that gives the board of directors or chief executive officers unbridled authority to make organizational decisions, formulate policies, and supervise the implementation. From there, directives, commands, and a modus operandi travels down a chain of command to employees.

Daniel Goleman (2001), in his book Primal Leadership, confirms that a 'top down' leadership approach relies 'heavily on getting employees to constantly ramp up efficiency and performance in meeting deadlines.' He emphasizes that 'while this approach may work in crunch time or aid others when information is to be provided urgently or immediately, it can wear on employees as a constant leadership style'. The 'valued' input of the recipients would certainly be embedded in the urgency, in which these directives, policies, and commands, will result in the desired outcomes, and more focused on the methods that will be employed to ensure stakeholders' compliance'.

This can make us leaders appear cold and distant. I have had instances in my leadership journey when I was accused of being cold and distant, only because I was ensuring crucial deadlines were met. I have also experienced sheer pressure during my most stressful moments, when the top executives' concern was not about my emotional well-being but the deliverables; ensuring that they receive the required information to complete their reports and submit them on time.

The top-down approach to leadership has convinced most leaders that their team works for them, giving them a sense of command and authority. They have been programmed to believe that effective leaders find a way to get their team members get the job done, without taking the most effective approach.

Sadly, it promotes the idea that leadership is a license to do less rather than a responsibility to do more (Simon Sinek). There is an unwritten guarantee that the proper execution of this approach offers opportunities for leaders to display their authority, competence, and expertise to get results and build followership, which is the employee's confidence in the leader.

In my opinion, this approach allows most leaders to watch things happen instead of making things happen. Regrettably, most employers have accepted this as the norm and accepted this as their leadership role and remain oblivious to the better side. They are content to be told what to do and how to do it. They accept the subtle exclusion, and unconsciously settle into thinking more of their limitations rather than potential.

This was a huge struggle at the start of my leadership journey. These perspectives troubled me on both sides. My experience has revealed that this can result in emotional frustration, stress, burnout, disengagement, and disgruntlement among employers and employees. I created my own balance that made me appear quite controversial to top executives, as well as some team members and stakeholders who in their own struggle, with their definition, and misunderstanding of leadership, constantly misinterpreted me.

Nonetheless, as a Christian leader, I overcame my struggles by having a meaningful conversation with myself, shifted my leadership mindset, and showed up differently by building a leadership habit as a servant leader.

I created a product and an undeniable brand of servant leader. I pride myself as an overcomer. I purposefully defy my leadership odds and model excellence by overcoming all challenges and keeping my focus on the ultimate goal of serving others. I remain inquiring, objectifying, logical, adaptable, compassionate, and kind in decision- making.

I do not mislead, exploit, or manipulate. (Proverbs 16: 10 – 20) highlights that God cares about honesty in the workplace; your business is his business. Christian leaders must abhor manipulation in all forms: sound leaders have a moral foundation. I lead with a servant mindset.

Aristotle once said, "He who cannot be a good follower cannot be a good leader." Thankfully, I have proven that in so many ways. Besides, God is the perfect model of servant leadership? He says, 'he who desires to be a leader must first be a servant'. Sadly, this leadership model is becoming extinct.

I have learned that great leaders are servant leaders, who often work from the back to get to the front or from the bottom up. They lead with empathy, coupled with a coaching mindset. They know that leadership is not about putting your passion into employees but allowing employees to buy into your vision and birth the passion in them.

Leadership is not about giving orders or demanding and rewarding compliance. It is also about listening and understanding. Although, understanding does not always equal tolerance, it promotes clarity, informed decision making, and accountability. Active listening involves empathy—the ability to set aside personal thoughts, feelings, and agendas in order to enter into another person's world. Such listening enables one to see other people's concerns from their perspectives.

According to Neil Kokemuller (2021), employees need to know that their leaders or employees care as much about them as they do about their work performance. When leaders lead with compassion, they 'show empathy for employees struggling with life challenges. They are more likely to create harmony and motivate workers to follow direction, even in tense company situations.

Empathy is highly beneficial in developing a team spirit but should be used wisely and intelligently to avoid inefficiency and poor discipline. Similarly, when leaders lead with a coaching mindset, they believe that they must lead by example with appreciative inquiry. They value feedback and see their primary responsibility as mentoring, training and developing workers to become their best self, set, and attain goals, and tap into their purpose at an optimal performance level.

Misunderstanding Leadership Roles

An offshoot to misunderstanding leadership is *misunderstanding your role as a leader.* When you choose to lead, you owe it to yourself and others to understand what it means. Many leaders misunderstand themselves as managers. They are more into managing everything else instead of finding ways to align and influence their team players and drive their spirit.

They pursue organizational goals through coordinated actions and tactical processes, or tasks and activities that unfold over stages to reach a certain outcome. An undeniable fact is that many mentors and supervisors are programmed to cultivate and amplify their managerial skills rather than leadership skills. However, management is not the fulcrum of leadership, it is influence.

Misunderstanding our leadership roles can inadvertently lead to self-imposed limitations under the guise of blind compliance. We tend to link specific "correct" actions or thoughts with our roles, and our perceptions of these roles, along with others' expectations. This not only shape our decisions and behavior but also influence our emotional responses to those choices (NHS).

In my opinion, the 'exceptional' leaders in today's workforce, and particularly the education industry, are perfect compliance officers. They administer and maintain established systems and structures, and never question or deviate from the plan of their superiors. They prefer not to take a risk that will result in change or disruption. They feel they must have the final word and think it is their job to deliver results every day. They also consider it their job to be the most knowledgeable, most capable, and most experienced member of the team. This is not true leadership.

Warren Bennis (2019) addresses this leadership deficiency with a firm declaration that "good leaders make people feel that they're at the very heart of things, not at the periphery." Philippians 2:3 reminds Christian leaders to 'do nothing out of selfish ambition, or vain conceit. Rather, in humility, value others above yourselves.' The greatest among you should be like the youngest and the one who leads like the one who serves (Luke 22:26).

True leaders 'are not afraid to be seen as vulnerable'. He pointed out that 'to be a great leader you have to leave your ego at the door'. He highlights a crucial point related to leadership roles which is that 'failing organizations are usually over-managed and under-led." True leadership demands that we confront injustice and the status quo, and not be content to be mirrors of other men's thoughts.

Warren Bennis (2020), who is widely regarded as a pioneer in the field of leadership studies, emphasizes the fact that "Leaders know the importance of having someone in their lives, who will unfailingly and fearlessly tell them the truth," and must do the same for their followers.

They must view their leadership role as being an accountability partner and not a manger. When they confuse the two, the leader becomes hooked on administering rather than innovating and developing talents, skills and abilities. They focus more on developing goals and the effective execution of these goals rather than enabling and driving change Dean Nitin Noria (2020). He concludes that 'If you act in a way that inspires, encourages, or engages others, you are a leader'.

Misunderstanding Training

Another mistake that leaders make is *misunderstanding training*. Paul, the apostle encourages the training of leaders. Paul travelled around the world to train up leaders and wrote letters to churches and leaders he did not have the liberty of going to. I also believe in training and development at all levels of an organization, but I believe that we must have something to show for it. Maria Jones (2019) statement, tell me and I'll forget, show me and I'll remember, involve me and I'll understand, or the Chinese adage, when I hear it, I forget it, when I see it, I remember, when I do it, I know it, jointly emphasize John Dewey thought that we learn more from doing than listening.

The truth is, misunderstanding our leadership roles can inadvertently lead to self-imposed obstacles under the guise of blind compliance. We tend to link specific "correct" actions or thoughts with our roles, and our perceptions of these roles, along with others' expectations, not only shape our decisions and behavior, but also influence our emotional responses to those choices (NHS).

Real training is not a show and tell; it involves simulation, trial and error and must be continuous, that the participant can be complete and equipped for good works (2 Tim. 3:17). P

Investing in training and consistent practice is essential, as practice indeed leads to improvement. Embracing responsive training helps build resilience against the misleading performance improvement doctrines that often rely on self-teaching from books, webinars, theories, one-day workshops, and PowerPoint presentations. These traditional approaches can prove to be expensive with limited tangible results within organizational settings.

Jeffrey Pfeiffer, a Stanford business school professor in his book Leadership BS, mentions that 'billions of dollars have gone into employee training and education, but they are not getting a good return on their investment'. He suggests that this is because we are training with pontifications and Venn diagrams that leaders cannot apply in the real world.

I have to agree. In the business industry, and especially the education industry of which I have served for over thirty-five years, we constantly mistake PowerPoints presentations, sensitization meeting, one-day workshops, seminars, and webinars as training models or programs. This wholesale misconception continues to take us on what has become a long and widening road from theory to practice. It has also weakened the trust in training programs or sessions that are carefully planned and intentionally created to provide the required practice and simulation for retention. In many instances, it has even resulted in cynicism and 'been there done that' syndrome. It is worth repeating for emphasis that, people need time and space to practice what they hear, see, and do for retention over the long term.

Many of the training programs that have swept through the education industry in my region are just fads. Of course, some have greater staying power than others because of the source, funding, and the apparent intent that coerce us into thinking that a particular program is valid and reasonable for the organization and the system because it will yield improved results.

Here is the fact: People learn differently and according to numerous learning models at their own pace. Each trainee's personal, practical sense of learning, and application is different. I have learned that no two individuals or organizations are the same. No two communities and families are the same. The context may be similar but not the same.

Training sessions are more effective when there are more similarities than differences.

Consequently, generic training models unfold within a complex set of conditions. The list of human and material variables is endless. The one-size-fits-all approach that organizational bureaucrat and top executives employ for expediency, emphasize their misunderstanding of training and the belief that 'training' is more important than the lasting value of preparation, understanding, developing expertise, and proper implementation.

In my context, training sessions usually fail because of insufficient simulation or the fact that you discover it cannot be applied in the real world. As a leader, you are told that you must 'motivate your team members', 'create a sense of vision' and 'see the bigger picture,' but you are not told exactly what to do.

Training must provide a step-by-step implementation plan. Of course, it must provide you theory along the way, but any training based on theory alone is already stamped for failure. It is very difficult for you to learn from a leader, instructor, or leadership model, if they do not have direct knowledge, experience, or understanding of your setting or context. It is always better and more beneficial to learn from somebody, who has proven that they have done your job successfully.

Another reason why training sessions fail is that the ideas presented look and sound great but are either too complicated or unworkable. This is because they are time consuming and require massive direct supervision demands that leaders do not have. Unless leaders have a capable assistant that will allow them to carve out the required time, the implementation is usually quite problematic; especially if it is a trial run for a doctoral thesis or training approach that is rooted in the theoretical passion of a technocrat and does not have an established procedural systematic outlay.

The final mistake that we make when training, which prevents training sessions from having the desired outcome is that the grassroots enforcers of the proposed training approach or model are not trained.

Most leadership initiatives require the buy in of team players and a change (no matter how small) in the organization's culture.

In many cases, leaders are the only ones who receive training, while those mandating the training often do not attend themselves. As a result, leaders find themselves in the position of having to explain and teach a new or desired approach that they themselves have not learned or fully understood, to those who are responsible for implementing real change. This disconnect can hinder the effective adoption of new practices within the organization.

The real hiccup is usually centered on an unsupportive organizational culture. If the new approach is not compatible with the organization's culture the process involved with changing the culture requires, time, energy and a particular sensitivity that is equally time consuming and more significantly can lead to a dead end. When all is said and done, responsive training allows each person at varying levels of the organization to be a worker who has no need to be ashamed and who is approved as rightly handling his or her role (2 Tim. 2:15).

Misunderstanding Motivation

Another mistake that we should avoid is *misunderstanding motivation.* Motivation should be important to a leader. As has been established in previous chapters, we are not arbitrarily appointed. We are purposefully commissioned. 'For we are God's handiwork, created in Christ Jesus to do good work, which God prepared in advanced for us to do', Ephesians 2:10.

It is important that as leaders we understand motivation and its impact. Why is it important for a leader to understand motivation? The simple answer would be that it helps you minimize disgruntlement, disengagement, and eliminate the 'undervalued syndrome' that rocks organizations. More importantly, it helps the leader to reward effort in an emotionally intelligent way.

Harappa (2021) says that 'motivation in an organization refers to the positive state of mind that drives you as a leader and your employees to achieve your objectives. Unless employees are happy, motivated, and incentivized, organizations are unlikely to perform well. Motivation in organizational behavior not only creates willingness but also encourages employees to fully utilize their abilities'.

Reeves (2015) explains that the reason many leaders misunderstand motivation is because of its dynamic nature. As humans, our motives constantly change to match our why, circumstances, and seasons. 'To further complicate matters, we are driven by a multitude of different motives at any one point in time'.

Reeves (2015) posits that at different times, one motive, usually the one most situationally appropriate, will be strongest and dominate our attention while other motives will be subordinate and lie relatively dormant. The strongest motive will have the most considerable influence on our behavior as our circumstances change. He also highlights that motivation is influenced by the satisfaction of needs that are either necessary for sustaining life or essential for wellbeing and growth. That said, motivation has as many faces as there are human desires Beata Souder's, (2019).

I have learned that every worker or person has his or her unique motivation language. Knowing our team members' expectations, beliefs and reference point is extremely important. There are many theories on motivation. However, I will briefly include only the motivational theories related to job satisfaction and dissatisfaction that influenced me and will assist me to develop my point. These theories provide a deeper understanding of how people behave and how to incentivize them to do better.

Victor Vroom's Expectancy Theory

Victor Vroom's (1960) expectancy theory of motivation proposes that an individual will behave or act in a certain way because they are motivated to select a specific behavior over others due to what they expect or desire the outcome to be.

In essence motivation is based on the value of the outcome, or if their role is perceived to be instrumental to the outcome. For example, an employee who desires a promotion or wants to be considered a prime candidate will go for an existing vacancy in your organization, may suddenly be willing to do over time, add previously undesirable tasks to his job description or offer valuable solutions for issues related to the new post. Leaders who understand this type of motivation are able to make better and wiser decisions related to employee engagement, and how to provoke one another to good works, Hebrews 10: 24.

Herzberg's Motivation- Hygiene Theory

Another theory that in my opinion adds value to this discussion is Herzberg's motivation-hygiene theory or dual-factor theory (1991). Herzberg argues that employee satisfaction has two dimensions; namely hygiene and motivation.

Motivators, such as recognition, achievement, the work itself, responsibility, advancement, and growth make workers more productive, creative and committed. Hygiene issues, such as company policy, interpersonal relations, working conditions, salary, and supervision cannot motivate employees but if handled properly can minimize dissatisfaction.

Addressing hygiene issues is essential to create a foundation for employee satisfaction, but it does not guarantee motivation. Contrary to the misconception that money is the primary motivator, creating a satisfying work environment is crucial for developing motivated, productive, and fulfilled team members.

Herzberg believed that to achieve success, organizations should strive to maintain a healthy balance between the two and consider how to spur one another on towards the desired outcome, Heb. 10:24.

Maslow's Theory of Human Motivation

Maslow's Theory of Human Motivation is another theory that affects or drives our decision-making at all levels of our personal and professional life. Maslow postulates that 'we are motivated when our basic needs are fulfilled'. As each foundational need and desire is met, it propels us to seek further fulfillment. For example, if an individual highly values work-life balance and is presented with a part-time opportunity, they will likely embrace it and commit to their responsibilities with utmost dedication.

According to Matthew Channel (2023), this theory is beneficial for leaders, as it will help them 'understand their employees' needs and provide them with a framework that motivates them toward positive discretionary behavior (that's doing positive things because they want to, not because they have to)'. He points out that leaders can help employees satisfy self-esteem and self-actualization needs by endeavoring to fulfil the most pressing needs at each level.

Those who yearn for and respond to the latter will be rewarded, Matt. 16:27

McClelland's Theory of Needs

David McClelland's Theory of Needs offers a profound perspective that, in my opinion, can revolutionize how leaders perceive motivation and the methods through which incentives are given and received. McClelland proposes three motivating drivers that shape our life experiences: achievement, affiliation, and power. Individuals with a high need for achievement are driven to pursue challenging goals and value recognition for their efforts.

On the other hand, some people are motivated by the social relationships they build and the positive interactions they engage in. Their need for affiliation drives them to excel in social settings and display exceptional interpersonal skills.

Lastly, individuals with a need for power aspire for roles that give them authority and actively wield their influence over others.

This theory has had a positive and personal impact on me. As a leader, I strongly believe in recognizing, validating, and rewarding effort and cultivating a positive culture of acknowledgement and appreciation.

During my leadership journey, I faced two situations in which team members remained dissatisfied even after receiving public recognition and rewards for their efforts. This theory served as an eye-opening revelation, helping me understand and communicate in their specific language of motivation. It offered essential insights into the factors that drive employees, which are crucial in a leading capacity to connect and engage with colleagues and team members.

It can also help identify the roots of conflicts and our faulty connections and promote healthier relationships. Paul, the apostle admonishes Christian leaders in the workplace,' if you owe someone respect, respect that person. If you owe someone honor, honor that person. Pay your debts as they come due' - Rom,13:7.

5 Motivational Language of Organizations

As a leader, I have come to understand that people's motivation varies based on factors like lifestyle factors, and environment. I have also realized that same people can react differently to a situation depending on the available incentives, their desired outcomes, and the timing.

According to Go Pivot in 2021, our society is driven by the need to succeed, and understanding what motivates us is crucial. It is evident that there is no one-size-fits-all approach to motivation and incentives.

People are driven by what they value, and often, it is a combination of several motivators. Some of us speak a combination of these motivational 'languages', with one being more dominant at times. Some of us transition between them depending on where we are in our lives' (Go Pivot, 2021).

Researchers have identified five motivational languages that influence decision-making in both our professional and daily lives. These languages include peer or leadership recognition, which provides a positive reinforcement and fosters a healthy team spirit.

Competition or gamification is another language that appeals to those who enjoy challenges and fun while working toward goals. Rewards satisfy individuals who need extrinsic motivators, with tangible rewards often proving more effective in maintaining motivation over the long term. The quality of life language resonates with those motivated by intrinsic factors, offering opportunities for personal growth and learning.

Lastly, the security, control, and power language appeals to individuals who value autonomy and the ability to contribute to organizational goals while maintaining a sense of security and importance.

These theories highlight a fact: there is no universal approach to motivation that suits everyone. One size certainly does not fit all.

For example, those seeking power and control will not find satisfaction in affiliation and rewards, regardless of their tangibility.

Employers can genuinely meet their employees' needs by comprehending and addressing their specific motivation language. As a Christian leader, it is essential to heed the guidance found in Ephesians 4:29, ensuring that words spoken are always constructive and tailored to meet the individual needs of those who listen.

Misunderstanding Feedback

Another mistake that leaders should avoid *is misinterpreting feedback*. Proverbs 15:33 highlights the power of feedback. 'If you reject discipline, you only harm yourself but if you listen to correction, you grow in understanding'. Feedback is a process of providing information or assessment to individuals or groups regarding their performance, behavior, or progress.

It is often misconstrued that when giving feedback, leaders should accentuate the positives and downplay the negatives, a practice referred to as the "feedback sandwich" by Pros sack (2019). However, wrapping negative feedback in praise can create a distorted picture of an individual's performance.

In reality, providing truthful yet positive negative feedback is essential. Leaders dedicated to a growth mindset invest time and effort in mastering the art of delivering negative feedback constructively.

Hence, it is entirely feasible to provide negative feedback positively without undermining the evaluation process. A leader with a growth- oriented mindset will devote the time and effort necessary to master the art of delivering constructive negative feedback.

As I progressed on my leadership journey, I had to learn, unlearn and relearn what I have been taught about feedback. Feedback is an inevitable component of leadership, often misunderstood due to its dynamic nature. The undeniable fact is that even the best of us are averse to feedback. Whether we want to accept it or not, many individuals perceive feedback as criticism or an assault, rather than an assessment or thorough examination of their strengths and areas of weaknesses.

On one hand, a performance evaluation, which is the ultimate method of providing feedback in many organizations, is often met with considerable apprehension, even when it is conducted with care, objectivity, gentleness, and amicability. In some cases, employees may go to the extent of taking sick leave to avoid it altogether. On the other hand, when feedback is dispensed inadequately, it can transform into a weapon of criticism rather than a tool of support.

Jennifer Porter (2019) categorically states that 'low-quality feedback is not useful, positive feedback is undervalued, and negative feedback delivered unskillfully can actually cause physical pain'.

She further highlights that 'unfortunately, the feedback that many leaders receive is not helpful because it is often infrequent, vague, or unrelated to specific behaviors. Truer words have never been spoken.

Effective feedback should be specific, consistent, timely, and actionable. Although we may sometimes feel a sense of reluctance towards evaluation, they are essential for helping individuals and teams within an organization to understand their strengths and weaknesses make improvements and achieve better results.

Many experts suggest that the frequency of feedback within an organization should be adaptable, considering factors like the specific situation, the nature of the work, and individual preferences. Regular, feedback is often advised over saving it for annual performance reviews.

These reviews should aim to foster constructive conversations rather than confrontations.

Leaders should be open to flexibility and adaptability, focusing on what is most effective for the organization and its members.

We must avoid relying on standardized conduct evaluation instruments that have remained unchanged for over a decade. In today's rapidly changing work environments and shifting organizational goals, these outdated tools can produce inaccurate data. This can lead to feedback that addresses past issues rather than the current needs of the organization. It is important to stay adaptable and ensure that the feedback process aligns with the organization's present requirements.

Another mistake to avoid relating to feedback is neglecting the person who needs feedback the most: the leader. In my role as an instructional leader, I developed an evaluation instrument for principals, and included sessions where my employees could provide me with feedback on my leadership roles and output. Encouraging them to be honest and candid in their feedback was a challenging task.

They were conditioned in previous settings to avoid actions or words that might upset their leaders due to fears of potential backlash.

Effective leaders benefit from feedback, which should flow in both directions. Potter (2019) highlights that 'everyone craves feedback,' emphasizing the importance of providing feedback meaningfully and collaboratively. When done poorly, review programs can lead to disengagement and wasted time.

Feedback can be categorized into three types: positive, reinforcing good behavior or performance, constructive (highlighting areas for improvement), and negative (addressing the positives). When dealing with poor performance, it is important to identify shortcomings and avoid harshness.

Feedback should be accompanied by a plan for growth, including support, training, and a personal improvement step. Employees facing performance issues must also be given a reasonable time to address the challenges, respond to help, guidance, and mentorship, and show improvement. It is important to promote self-reflection, self-awareness, and self-regulation, and other practical suggestions after offering feedback.

A leader should not provide a fix. In challenges like meeting deadlines, leaders should suggest self-management strategies or provide a coach for overcoming obstacles. When employees struggle in new roles, leaders should avoid judgment and encourage them to explore their challenges. Instead of offering personal solutions, recommend support and training based on their needs.

Finally, feedback is most beneficial when it fosters a sense of value, involving both team members and leaders. This allows for honest assessments to identify weaknesses and strengths. Effective feedback must provide direction, motivation, performance improvement, and mutual engagement. If feedback does not tick all these boxes, it is merely criticism, complaining, and not genuine feedback.

In summary, feedback is a vital tool for leaders and organizations to promote growth, enhance performance, and maintain effective communication. Different types of feedback serve various purposes, with benefits like improved performance, increased motivation, and stronger teamwork.

Misunderstanding Delegation

Delegation is a valuable practice, as even in Numbers 11:17, God advised Moses to delegate tasks and share the burden. However, the power of delegation can be misused when seen as forced labor. Many diligent leaders misunderstand delegation due to industry pressures. It is crucial to realize that as you move up the ranks, effective delegation becomes even more important. Consequently, as a leader you may have been verbally and mentally trained to offload tasks and responsibilities, but not authority to other individuals or teams to achieve specific goals. As a result, leaders often become data clerks and compliance wardens, primarily focused on gathering information for reporting. When leaders express stress, become overwhelmed, or show signs of burnout, they are repeatedly advised to learn how to delegate.

Time after time when real issues are presented for collaborative solutions, they are often brushed aside with words like,' you must learn the art of delegating'. I can recall during my early days as a leader that my top executives emphasized the importance of a leader's ability to delegate effectively.

Delegation is often misunderstood as a simple act of passing on tasks and responsibilities to subordinates, but it is more complex than that. It is about assigning the right people who can handle tasks effectively. This can be quite bothersome in a small organization.

I have learnt as a leader that delegation does not always work as intended and there are several reasons why this is so. Firstly, it requires careful planning, open communication, and a willingness to trust and empower your team members.

Delegation is a critical aspect of effective leadership, and it is not about dictation but distributing formal authority. If tasks are not delegated, the team can become inefficient and demoralized. However, unclear objectives and ambiguous instructions can lead to confusion among those tasked.

Delegation can fail if the individuals or teams receiving the task are not adequately trained, leading to wasted time and resources, as well as frustration. Poor communication and micromanagement can hinder delegation as well. When leaders overly supervise delegated tasks, it can stifle motivation and autonomy, leading to resentment among employees who feel untrusted. Poor communication can result in missed deadlines and a misalignment of expectations. Another important aspect of delegation is the follow up. Delegation should not be treated as a one-time action.

It requires ongoing support, guidance, and feedback. If a leader does not follow up or aid when needed, many things can go wrong.

Similarly, delegating tons of tasks to one person or team should also be avoided, as it leads to overload, burnout, reduced quality, missed deadlines, lack of motivation, disengagement, and frustration.

Knowing when to delegate is another crucial skill for effective leaders. Delegating is particularly helpful when:

- The task offers valuable training to the individual.
- An employee has more expertise or experience related to the task than needs to be done.
- When the task is recurring, and all employees need training and preparation.
- When you need or should have a backup.
- When the task is low priority and you have high priority tasks that require your immediate attention.

All in all, to make delegation work effectively leaders need to:

- Clearly define the tasks, objectives, and expectations.
- Match the right person or team with the task based on skills and interests.
- Provide the necessary resources, training, and support.
- Communicate regularly and maintain an open line of communication.
- Trust the individuals or teams to complete the tasks.

- Follow up at appropriate intervals to monitor progress.
- Offer constructive feedback and recognize small achievements.

God in Eph. 5: 8-17 reminds Christian leaders:

'you were once in darkness, but now you are light in the Lord. Walk as [leaders] of light'.

Leaders should be open to learning from their delegation experiences, both successful and unsuccessful, and use that knowledge to refine their delegation approach in the future.

Delegation is a skill that improves with practice, inquiry, and good judgment. Christian leaders must learn to master this skill by recognizing their own limitations and their team members' potential.

Effective delegation is a valuable tool for leaders, as it enhances productivity, fosters employee development, and contributes to overall organizational success.

'See then that you walk circumspectly, not as fools but as wise.'

Misunderstanding Succession Planning

Many organizations make the mistake of *misunderstanding succession planning*. Given that this book is addressed to Christian leaders in a

professional workplace, I want to set the framework

for discussion. God is a fan of succession planning.

There are numerous instances in the bible where God emphasizes the power of succession planning. In 1Kings 19:16 -21, God asked Elijah to anoint Elisha as a successor. Numbers 27:16 tells the story of Joshua, who was groomed to succeed Moses, and the gospels tell the story of how Jesus' disciples were prepared to complete His mission.

In fact, they were commissioned and given a divine command to continue the good work he started. Thus, I believe that having a succession plan is God's will.

He has shown us the importance of good succession planning. One common mistake leader make is delaying succession planning, often when things are running smoothly and there are capable middle managers and group leaders.

Succession planning is often underestimated. Just because someone is capable and bright does not mean they are automatically prepared to fill a leadership role when the time comes.

Effective leaders know that developing a successor involves meticulous, behind-the-scenes work not found in a manual. A well- implemented succession plan creates a deep bench of potential leaders. This provides the appropriate flexibility and the flexibility of choosing the most suitable candidate for a given situation.

I recognize a succession plan as a powerful stabilizer. Without a succession plan, leadership vacancies can create uncertainty and risk.

Human Resource managers emphasizes the need for 'orderly transitions of authority' to build a sustainable organization.

Without continuity, people become confused and fearful, work structures fall apart, and workers become ineffective.' Let me insert a timely reminder that even with a succession plan, limiting your succession plan to just some members of your team or neglecting to set timelines for completion is also a huge mistake that must be avoided.

An effective plan should nurture a group of future leaders, promote inclusivity, and offer opportunities for a diverse group of individuals that fit different leadership positions. Great leaders initiate successor development in advance to make a graceful departure in the future.

Numbers 27:16, points out that the institutions, whether big or small, need effective processes for training and succession. Another drawback of faulty succession planning is that some leaders feel that they must secretly develop internal talents by confidentially preparing a team of their own. This is a big mistake. One individual may not know everything. Succession planning is the responsibility of both the current executive, and those who exercise complimentary authority.

Effective succession planning involves developing the right leaders for the right roles, ensuring good decision-making, high morale, and preserving institutional knowledge. It aligns leadership development with an organization's strategic goals, preparing future leaders to execute its vision and strategy.

Succession planning relies on people, and their mindsets and personality traits can influence its success. Some may resist assigned responsibilities, seeing the leader as lazy, unreasonable, or unfair. We should acknowledge this potential challenge and address it with understanding and communication.

In a personal experience, one of my capable team members, after successfully completing assigned tasks, mistakenly claimed to be doing my job. I addressed this by asking her to compare my job description with her actual assigned tasks. She realized she was not performing any of my responsibilities, and we resolved the situation.

The important points to remember from this discussion are:

- Succession planning is essential but can be a tricky process.
  We cannot think of succession planning only when a leadership role needs to be filled.
- We cannot elect a successor based on familiarity or haste.

☒ We cannot consider just one person for a position we should identify and train multiple successors, internally and externally.

☒ We shouldn't choose employees based on their current role performance but rather their ability to train and support, as well as their expertise and consistency.

A succession plan is a fail if it excludes key stakeholders or if the succession planning process is not transparent or effectively communicated to all key stakeholders.

Misunderstanding Resilience The Final Mistake

Leaders sometimes mistake "bouncing back" for real resilience. As Christian leaders, we need to discuss this because in our context, it is easy to misunderstand resilience. God created us to be resilient while recognizing our humanity.

As Christian leaders, we trust in God and have faith that we can rely on His strength. Our faith makes us resilient. We can endure difficult situations, knowing we are not alone, and find meaning in them, trusting that God works everything together for our good.

In that breath, 'he wishes above all that we should prosper and be in good health' 3 John 1:2.

Some leaders may equate resilience solely with the ability to endure hardship without breaking down. They might consider employees that can handle high levels of stress, while maintaining productivity. Even though, those individuals are actually suffering from burnout or chronic stress. This misconception can lead to long-term negative consequences for both individuals and organizations. In certain industries like education and healthcare, leaders may unintentionally promote resilience at any cost, creating a culture where employees feel pressured to hide their struggles and avoid seeking help when needed, ultimately harming their well-being.

Some leaders mistakenly believe that resilience means returning to the same level of performance after facing adversity or a crisis, which is unrealistic. In reality, true resilience often leads to personal growth and development. From my experiences, I have learned that no one emerges from a crisis the same; there is often a shift in mindset and behavior. When employees are given the space to adapt positively and learn from their experiences, they become resilient over time.

Resilience goes beyond mental or physical toughness; it also encompasses emotional well- being. Many leaders tend to prioritize task completion and meeting deadlines while overlooking employees' emotional needs.

Employees may endure their situation while silently looking for an escape and leaders can misinterpret this as resilience.

Leaders who lead with compassion and kindness recognize their obligation to introduce proactive measures to prevent or mitigate the impact of challenges. These measures can also serve to prevent the cycle of repeated setbacks and treat the underlying vulnerabilities and issues.

Leaders who depend on their perceptions of how well their team navigates adversity often overlook opportunities to build resilience through training, mental health support, and stress management programs.

True resilience, from the organization's perspective, includes both individuals' adaptability and the organization's support during challenging times. To prevent misconceptions about resilience, leaders should practice appreciative inquiry, pay attention to unspoken concerns, and take a multi-dimensional approach to enhance the overall well-being of their team members.

Key takeaways from this discussion are:

⊠ Resilience is a dynamic and multi- dimensional concept.
⊠ Resilience should not be confused with bouncing back, as it goes beyond returning to the previous state before adversity.
⊠ True resilience includes emotional well- being, personal growth, and the creation of supportive environments for individuals to thrive despite challenges.

In summary, building resilience involves learning from adversity, making positive changes to prevent future challenges, and addressing the emotional and psychological aspects of difficulties in a supportive environment. As you reflect on this chapter, ask yourself these questions:

As a leader what are the mistakes I am making?

What aspects of my leadership am I misunderstanding due to faulty programming?

What do I need to unlearn, relearn, and learn to show up differently?

How do my personality traits influence my leadership style?

Leadership nugget

When we are no longer able to change a situation, we are challenged to change ourselves. (Viktor E. Frankl)

Let us pray:

Dear God,

Give me the courage to admit when I do wrong. I seek your guidance and your direction in every decision. Help me lead with wisdom, integrity, and a heart of compassion. Amen

Chapter 12

Personality Types -Traits and Leadership

'Make a careful exploration of who you are and the work that you have been given, and then sink yourself into that. Do not be impressed with yourself. Don't compare yourself to others.'(Gal.6: 4).

Throughout my leadership journey, I have encountered numerous personality clashes. These clashes are not indicative of poor leadership; rather, they stem from being an effective leader with a balanced mix of results- oriented, data-driven, compassionate, kind, firm, emotional intelligence, and authentically servant-oriented traits.

Each clash has propelled me into deep self-reflection, bringing me closer to my purpose, core values, uniqueness, and a heightened self- awareness regarding my adaptation, flexibility matrix, communication styles, and my non- negotiables.

In the first chapter of this book, I emphasized my personal philosophy that governs my behavior, decision-making, and shapes my personal and professional actions. I restate it here to strengthen the pillar of my discussion: 'The greatest want of the world is the want of men who will not be bought or sold. Men who in their inmost souls are true and honest. Men who do not fear to call sin by its right name. Men whose conscience is as true to duty as the needle to the pole. Men who will stand for the right though the heavens fall" (Ellen G. White, Education, p.4).

This philosophy serves as my guiding 'bible verse' of authentic leadership, a resounding reference point throughout my leadership journey, shaping my experiences – both positive and challenging, guiding me through wilderness experiences, and helping me navigate the complexities and misunderstandings of leadership.

The personality clashes prompted me to explore my personality traits and examine my leadership style. This self-examination also involved understanding the dynamics of how I interact with individuals in my organization and how they, in turn, affect me.

I have discovered that separating a leader's personality from their leadership style is a myth. Leadership is not just what we do; it is also who we are, why we are, and how we are.

Thus, I agree with Jim Clemmer (2021) that some people are good leadership performers. They can "do their leadership thing" and put on very convincing acts; but in time, superficial leadership wears thin.

People see through the act and authenticity suffers. Superficial leadership is a motivation spoiler that ultimately erodes trust and drains energy, leading to feelings of manipulation, cynicism, and suspicion. In such a climate, stronger inducements or threats may be necessary to compel others to comply. Clemmer, rightly emphasizes that the most profound and enduring leadership comes from within – it is authentic, genuine, and true.

Author and consultant Robert Cooper (2019) refer to this as a leader's 'authentic presence.' It means that 'moment by moment, the emotional truth of who you really are, deep down, and what you stand for, care about, and believe. When you live from the depths of the heart, you walk your talk, heed your conscience, and don't hesitate to take a stand.'

That is why I embrace authentic leadership and include this chapter.

It is important for a leader to comprehend not only their personality traits but also those of their team members or employees. According to Marcia Nerine Weldon (2021), 'a leader who understands their strengths and communication style, and more importantly, understands their team's strengths and communication styles, is exponentially more effective.'

Rita Sinha's (2021) idea about leadership explains that each leader has a unique footprint created by their personality and talent. A leader's personality and talent influence how they perform and lead for better or for worse. This footprint has the power to build a personal and organizational legacy. Mindful leaders use it to achieve their goal, shape their organizational culture and create the desired employee experience.

Understanding Personality Types and Traits

As I matured as a leader and confronted personality clashes, my Christian faith led me to engage in introspective dialogues. I acknowledge that achieving peace with everyone is a two- sided endeavor that borders on impossible, but I still hold onto the biblical principle: 'if it is possible, as much as it depends on me, I am to live peacefully with all men'- (Romans. 12:18).

I observed that most of my personality clashes were with stakeholders and individuals who exhibit a fixed mindset, manipulative or calculating streak, sought constant attention, made unreasonable demands, and prioritized self-gratification over cooperate responsibility or accountability.

I firmly believe that no one individual should

constantly seek the spotlight. Every person within an organization plays a crucial role in its success, and all roles should be treated with equal respect and dignity. Each member of the organization deserves recognition and acknowledgment when their time to shine comes.

I was inspired to delve into research on personality types and traits due to the actions of two team members who intended to create division among my employees. They attempted to sow discord by distinguishing between old and new staff and using the challenges faced by new employees in adapting to the demanding environment they had subtly fostered, as a source of complaints. They initially labeled it as uncooperativeness, later shifting to the perceived unwillingness of new employees to accept constructive criticism.

As an experienced leader in my industry and a certified life coach, I had a good understanding of the four basic personality types, and a working knowledge of personality traits. However, when this situation escalated into an ongoing problem, it drove me to a more thorough investigation.

Consequently, I sought answers from research and my overarching mandate as a Christian leader, which also led me to seek a biblical perspective. I asked essential questions that I encourage you to contemplate and answer as you read this chapter.

How are personality types different from personality traits?

My research led me to several theories about personality types and traits. According to Wikipedia:

Personality type typically refer to a broad category or classification of an individual based on certain shared characteristics and tendencies. The Myers-Briggs Type Indicator (MBTI) (2017), presents 16 personality types based on combinations of four dichotomous preferences namely extraversion vs introversion and thinking vs feeling. They note that personality types are often seen as discrete categories that place individuals into one of these types.

Carl Nielson (1902) Four Temperament Theory suggests that there are four fundamental personality types, sanguine, choleric, phlegmatic and melancholy. Although his theory does not find favor with modern psychology, I want to discuss this theory because it continues to be relevant and is an excellent starting point for aspiring, beginning and executive leaders to begin to understand and response to the different personality types and traits of their employees.

Carly Gail (2021) emphasizes that that 'when a leader doesn't acknowledge that their team is comprised of unique individuals with different personalities trouble is sure to ensue'. She explains that our personality affect how we react to our situations, work more efficiently, resolve conflict, communicate and more.

'Because personality dictates people's behavior, leaders must understand the types of their team members.

Through deliberate and purposeful observations, comparisons, and application of gathered information, I classified my team members based on personality type, observable personality traits and their nature of communicating to effectively manage and gradually minimize future personality clashes.

I maintained a mental diary, reminding me of each team member's personality traits, communication preferences, and other characteristics. In other words, I knew who was choleric, sanguine, phlegmatic, and melancholic; as well as their preferences for praise, tangible rewards, recognition, authority, and more.

For example, a sanguine personality type is extroverted, optimistic, energetic talkative, impulsive, and adaptable. As leaders, they are good at motivating and inspiring their team.

They excel in social situations, are natural communicators, and build strong relationships with team members. The main weakness is that this individual lack self-control, and often act on feelings and desires without much thought. Consequently, as a leader, they may need assistance with long term planning and organization.

On the other hand, a choleric personality type is goal-oriented, decisive, impatient, assertive, independent, and dominant. These leaders are results-driven and excel in roles where decisiveness and assertiveness are essential.

They can make tough decisions quickly and drive projects forward. However, they may prefer to work alone and struggle with taking instructions, so developing interpersonal skills and sensitivity to others' needs to crucial for them as leaders.

The phlegmatic personality type is characterized by calmness, patience, empathy, and an aversion to conflict. As leaders, they are skilled at maintaining harmony within their teams.

They are patient, empathetic, and approachable, making them good at resolving conflicts and creating a supportive work environment. Their main weakness is indecisiveness, as they may have difficulty making decisions and can be passive. To become more effective leaders, they need to work on assertiveness and making necessary decisions.

The melancholic personality type is introverted, analytical thinking, perfectionism, emotionally sensitivity, reservation, and caution.

As leaders, they are often thorough and precise in their work. They excel at planning, analysis, and paying close attention to details. They can provide stability and structure to their teams. Their main weakness is that these individuals make decisions slowly are afraid to take risks and are deeply affected by their experiences. As leaders, they may struggle with delegating tasks and sometimes exhibit excessive criticism.

Many individuals exhibit a combination of these personality traits while maintaining a dominant temperament category. It is important for leaders to recognize these traits in their team members and adapt their leadership approach accordingly.

If we are to evaluate these personality types from a biblical perspective, we see numerous leaders in the bible who demonstrated these personality types and whose personality type influenced their performance. For example, bible scholars express the thought that Peter was sanguine because he was brash and impulsive and often spoke and acted without thinking. He demonstrated this in the garden of Gethsemane, walking on water and denying Christ after making strong declarations of loyalty – (Matt.14): 22-33.

Drawing connections between personality types

and biblical figures can provide a fresh perspective on these well-known stories.

Identifying Moses as a melancholic leader based on his inclination toward what was right and his responses to conflicts is an interesting interpretation. It highlights how our understanding of personality traits can add depth to our understanding of historical and biblical figures.

The apostle Paul appeared to be choleric because of how focused he was on his goal, and how tirelessly he worked at achieving his goals without fear or favor – Corinthians 15:10.

The example of Deborah, the only female judge mentioned in the scriptures, is a fascinating addition to the discussion of personality types. Describing her as having the easy-going, peace- promoting personality traits of a phlegmatic offer a unique perspective on her leadership style. It is a great way to connect personality types with biblical figures and their leadership roles.

In being a great leader, the first step is self-awareness and the willingness to adapt and grow. Understanding your personality strengths, weaknesses, and leadership style is a great way to foster the most effective leadership in your position.

The Big Five Model of personality traits is indeed

a widely recognized and extensively studied framework for understanding personality. It identifies five key personality traits: openness, conscientiousness, extraversion, agreeableness, and neuroticism. Each individual fall somewhere along a spectrum for each of these traits, with varying degrees or scores. It is a valuable tool for assessing and understanding an individual's personality characteristics.

Openness to experience is a personality trait that reflects an individual's willingness to embrace new experiences and ideas. People at the high end of this trait tend to be curious, creative, open to their emotions, appreciative of beauty, and eager to explore new things. In contrast, those at the lower end of the scale are more likely to be traditional and resistant to change, often preferring stability and familiarity.

Conscientiousness is a personality trait that reflects an individual's level of self-discipline, organization, and goal-oriented behavior. Those with high conscientiousness are typically organized, self-disciplined, and strive for achievement, often adhering to duties and expectations. On the other hand, individuals at the lower end of the conscientiousness spectrum may be more spontaneous, extravagant, and less concerned with organization and self-discipline. They might appear careless or disorganized in their approach to tasks and responsibilities.

Extraversion trait is marked as outgoing or energetic at the high end of the scale. Extraverts are enthusiastic and action-oriented. They possess high group visibility, like to talk, and assert themselves as opposed to introverts who are at the low end and prefer a more solitary, less stimulating or reserved environment.

Agreeableness is a strong personality trait within the Big Five personality traits.

They are considered considerate, kind, generous, trusting, helpful, and willing to compromise.

They tend to be optimistic about human nature. On the other hand, those with low agreeableness prioritize self-interest over getting along with others. They may be skeptical about others' motives, leading to suspicion, unfriendliness, and uncooperativeness.

Neuroticism is a well-studied temperament trait. It involves experiencing strong negative emotions like anger, anxiety, or depression. People high in neuroticism are emotionally reactive and easily stressed. They often interpret everyday situations as threatening and may find minor issues overwhelmingly difficult. Their negative emotions linger for extended periods, leading to frequent bad moods. On the other hand, individuals with low neuroticism are less easily upset, emotionally stable, and generally free from persistent negative feelings.

Our personality has a significant impact on how we lead. In the Bible, there are numerous leaders, whose personality traits and talents enhanced their ministry and many whose personality trait contributed to their failure as a leader.

One such exemplary leader is Noah. Noah's conscientiousness trait allowed him to accept the unpopular assignment to build an ark.

Although, ridiculed, maligned, and insulted, Noah was isolated, lonely but obedient to God's command to build an ark (boat). His unwavering faith and resilient personality trait make him stand out to this day as the man who instigated the first flood and who single handedly saved the entire race.

Another worthy example is Joseph who is very high on the agreeableness scale. Joseph's positive and forgiving attitude, driven by his high level of agreeableness, is a key aspect of his leadership. Despite challenges and mistreatment, he remained optimistic and forgiving, which ultimately led to his rise to a position of authority in Egypt. This illustrates how personality traits can shape one's leadership journey.

Moses, who was on the high end of openness to new experiences, and Job, who was on the low end, both demonstrated remarkable patience and resilience. Leading millions of complaining people through a desert for 40 years is no small feat, but Moses did it calmly and confidently.

Job endured numerous setbacks and losses, relying on his personality traits and beliefs to remain steadfast. Moses effectively prepared Joshua to succeed him as a leader, and Joshua's courage, perseverance, and guidance from God led to his success. David, a young man with extraordinary courage and wit, faced and defeated Goliath in battle, trusting in God's protection because he believed he was chosen by God.

Daniel, who is high on the conscientiousness scale, proved himself to be a man of integrity. Despite multiple tests and threats to his faith in God, the king's diet, a golden statue, a lions' den, he demonstrated unwavering integrity and service to God.

John, a prominent biblical figure known for his outspoken and brutally honest character, set a crucial precedent for uprightness and moral leadership, a quality often lacking in many 21st- century leaders.

Paul shared similarities with John in his outspokenness and brutal honesty, displaying traits associated with high extraversion. He was deeply passionate and fiercely loyal to the cause he supported. Paul's willingness to admit when he was wrong and his prolific writings, played a significant role in shaping the beliefs and culture of the modern world.

They were often angry or anxious, and their negative emotional reactions persisted, keeping them in a bad mood. Tragically, their stubborn and pigheaded personality traits contributed to their failure as leaders and ultimately led to their untimely demise.

Personality and leadership are closely intertwined, as a leader's personality traits can significantly influence the leadership style and your effectiveness as a leader. Effective leadership involves recognizing one's strengths and weaknesses, then adapting their approach to align with the organization's goals and mission. The key is understanding how your personality traits can best serve your leadership role.

It is important to remember this when thinking about the quality of your leadership and its impact on the employees. As Susan Sadler suggests, leaders should have a deep understanding of what works for them and what hinders their effectiveness. This self-awareness should encompass core beliefs, cultural influences, and how these factors shape one's leadership style. Ultimately, you have the power to decide how you want to be recognized as a leader.

Do my personality traits shape my approach to leading?

Different personality traits can shape a leader's approach to leading their team or organization. Natasha Ganev (2021) affirms that a leader's personality informs whether they work hard or skirt the details, diffuse conflict or escalate it, listen and engage with intention or refuse to stay curious and grateful. For example, strong-willed and assertive individuals may adopt an authoritative style, making decisions with little input from others.

However, democratic leaders with a more open and inclusive personality may employ a participative role that involves team members in decision making. Transformational leader's charismatic and visionary personality often inspire and motivate their teams to achieve shared goals. Lastly, servant leaders empathetic and compassionate personality focus on serving the needs of their team members and empowering them to excel.

Another intriguing side of personality trait is our ability to adapt and evolve as leaders based on our personality traits. A leader who tends to worry may be highly cautious and focused on potential risks and challenges, and thus, demonstrates a strong sense of responsibility, careful planning and keen foresight based on intense analysis. However, excessive worrying can result in analysis paralysis, indecisiveness and a lack of adaptability.

A leader with a critical approach often pays close attention to details and is particularly skilled at identifying areas of improvement, often provide constructive feedback and drive team members to constantly strive for excellence. The thing is criticism must be balanced and specific. Excessive criticism may lead to a negative work environment and low morale.

Then there is the leader who displays victim-like tendencies who struggle with taking responsibility and ownership for decisions and actions. I believe that a leader should be resilient, accountable and willing to face challenges head-on. A leader who views him/herself as a victim hinders his/her ability to effectively lead and inspire team members. A perfectionist leader holds him/herself and team members to very high standards, has an eye for detail and a strong desire to achieve flawless outcomes. These traits can be highly beneficial as they can lead to high-quality work, however it might also result in undue stress, micromanagement, and difficulty in delegating tasks.

A leader who is concerned with building is focused on growth, innovation, and creating opportunities, is visionary and proactive and is always looking for ways to expand and improve the organization. His/her visionary and proactive traits and knack for turning ideas into reality can fix his/her attention on achieving goals and isolate or ignore the needs of team member who are unenthusiastic or struggle to keep up.

A leader with a fixer mentality usually excels at problem solving and addresses issues as they arise. They have a practical and hands on approach to challenges and very adept at handling crises. Their main issue is that they focus too much on short-term fixes rather than long-term solutions.

A leader who is a breaker may challenge the status quo and traditional norms and policies especially if they are considered outdated or oppressive. They are extremely comfortable with change and disruption and often push boundaries to drive innovation and transformation. While this trait can lead to breakthroughs, it might also create resistance or instability if not managed carefully.

A leader who prioritizes maintenance is dedicated to stability, consistency and preserving what already works well. He/she is focused on ensuring that processes are efficient, risks are minimized, and the organization's foundation remains strong. An excessive focus on maintenance often hinders adaptability and growth.

That said, it would be foolhardy to a leader embodies just one of these characteristics. The fact is that as a leader you often display more than one of these characteristics at given times. The main thing is that a successful leader knows when to emphasize certain traits based on the context, situation and the needs of the team or organization. Adapting and evolving these qualities, as circumstances change is key to becoming a well-rounded and effective leader.

How do personality traits affect my interpersonal relationships?

Leaders fulfill a variety of roles that contribute to the overall success of their team and organization. These roles often involve interpersonal skills, strategic thinking, and the ability to inspire and motivate. As a leader, your personality affects how you communicate with your team. If you possess excellent interpersonal skills, such as empathy and active listening, you tend to build strong connections with your team members and understand their needs better.

Your personality traits also influence your level of emotional intelligence, which is crucial for effective leadership. If you possess a high EI, you are able to manage your emotions and help your teammates to manage theirs, understand and empathize with others and handle conflicts more effectively.

Your personality trait also affects how you approaches decision-making. You may be an analytical, data driven and results oriented leader while your key team members in decision- making might rely on intuition and gut feelings. Personality types that are high on conscientiousness or who have a choleric personality is likely to get frustrated while waiting on your teammates to catch up.

Leaders with a diplomatic and patient personality are often better equipped to handle conflicts within their teams and find mutually beneficial solutions. As a leader, your personality trait can also determine how you handle challenges and setbacks and how you motivate your team to overcome them.

Your personality type as a leader can also influence how you inspire and motivate your team to buy into your vision and strategize to achieve organizational goals. It can contribute or take away from team spirit and prevent or mobilize team members to achieve remarkable results.

In summarizing. Caitlin Meyer (2022) asserts

that identifying one's own dominant traits and those of others can improve communication and collaboration, leading to relationships that are more effective and ultimately better results.

How do leaders align personality traits of team members with organizational tasks or roles?

I feel the need to end this chapter with this question as a feel it is like an elephant in the room. Besides, of what practical use would this knowledge be if it could not be applied in real life settings'?

Therefore, I want to give some practical guidelines that is confirmed by research combined with a unique blend of qualifications, experience, expertise and research. Caitlin Meyer (2022) an expert in psychological science and registered Psychometrist says, 'we all exhibit a variety of different behavioral styles [and that] an awareness of our behavioral preferences can accelerate career progression and organizational productivity. This is another relevant side of personality traits and style that I think is often unheard. Therefore, I could not close this chapter without including a wholesome discussion on the original and most widely accepted theory of personality and behavior, the 'DISC' theory.

This theory originated in 1928 when William Moulton Marston published "Emotions of

Normal People." In this book, Marston outlined his research into human behavior. He asserts that a person's behavior is based on an individual's perception of and reaction to a situation. Using this theory Thomas (1958) created the DISC behavioral assessment, which is one of the most valid psychometric assessments and is rated as most highly effective to understand an individual's behavior in the workplace. The insights gained from the DISC behavioral assessment empower individuals and organizations with a greater level of understanding of their capabilities, behavioral alignment with a task or role, likely contribution to their team and their reactions and response to pressure.

Marston (1928) grouped these reactions into four major behavioral types or styles, which are sometimes referred to as 'DISC behavioral types. The four types are: D – Dominance, I – Influence, S – Steadiness and C – Compliance. Using the words of Caitlin Meyer (2022), People who have high 'dominance' in their behavioral profiles are results driven. They are focused on expediting action, comfortable with challenge, and very decisive. 'Based on their drive to succeed, they may also be highly conscientious, the trait that most strongly predisposes an individual to succeed at work' (Macrae). Although they are motivated by autonomy and challenge, they are likely to become frustrated when excessive challenges impede the delivery of results.

However, people with a predominantly 'influential' behavioral style are motivated by their effect on others. They are adept at forming and cultivating relationships, generating enthusiasm in co-workers, and often radiate optimism. Animated and enthusiastic, influencers are motivated by building relationships and communicating ideas. They are verbal, they are natural networkers and shine in discussions, gaining commitment from others, boosting morale and cultivating relationships. Sadly, they struggle to maintain motivation should they lose access to the social connection and approbation that motivates them. They may also struggle to maintain concentration if working in isolation for long periods without the opportunity to collaborate with others.

Conversely, people with 'steadiness' as a working strength deliver consistently through processes and teamwork. They tend to focus on the job at hand and diligently see work projects through to completion. They take a methodical approach to managing their workload and can persist where other personality styles might more quickly become distracted or lose interest. Notably, team members who are high in steadiness can help to stabilize teams that are undergoing change.

However, people with this personality trait can be disruptive and demotivated by rapid changes in their working environment.

People with 'compliance' as a working strength are excellent fact-checkers and risk assessors. They are detail oriented and are typically focused on maintaining and improving standards, analyzing information and monitoring and controlling quality. They have a similar reaction as individuals of the steadiness type, as they can be easily derailed by disruption to existing systems than other types. High change work settings may be stressful and ultimately demotivating for people with this behavioral preference. However, compliance is also critical to successfully managing change, contributing in-depth analyses, enforcing quality standards, assessing risk and exercising diplomacy

What I find most appealing about Thomas (1958) behavior assessment theory, is that the information garnered can be used to enhance personal and organizational performance in a number of areas. These include understanding employees' inherent motivation, preferred communication style, enhancing peer and team interactions, identifying teammates' strengths and weaknesses, and informing decision- making.

Marston's theory plots human behavior along two dimensions: 'internal' and 'external', which he notes, interact to produce the four different behavioral types, or modes of expression. His theory stated that our behavior is determined by whether we perceive our environment to be essentially antagonistic or favorable, and whether we choose to adopt an active or passive response to it.

A wise leader articulates and owns one's personality and unique talents, as well as the other sides of these traits. In fact, this is necessary for leaders, as it not only allows them to 'utilize more of their natural strengths to get help with areas they are not wired for' but also helps them to 'avoid repeating the unhelpful patterns that could affect their well-being or relationships.

'A key benefit of understanding one's personality preferences is that leaders can be more aware and accepting of how other people are different. This allows them to proactively flex their leadership style to get the best out of others. For example, a leader who is 'outcome-focused' can demotivate a person who is 'people focused.' By being more emphatic, they can engage and inspire this person instead.' Gabriella Goddard (2021)

As a Christian leading in a professional space my interaction with the Thomas DISC behavior assessment was mostly beneficial in an understanding of how I can proactively assign tasks and responsibilities to team members in accordance with their personality traits and behavioral predispositions. My goal was twofold. On one hand, I wanted to use what I do best, to do what I love, to produce results that matter.

On the other hand, I wanted to meaningfully help my teammates to harness their talents and capabilities and serve from a place of wholeness, clarity and confidence.

So, what did I learn from these theories and how did I apply it in my leadership setting?

Putting It All Together

In this chapter we learnt that there are generally four personality types: sanguine, melancholy, choleric and phlegmatic; there are up to sixteen personality traits categorized into five main categories; openness, conscientiousness, extraversion, agreeableness and neuroticism and that individuals respond in the workplace using four behavioral types or styles, dominance, influence, steadiness and compliance (DISC).

When I put it all together, I find that they are all connected and has an abiding theme; Expertise and knowledge is simply not enough. A leader with a personality that is not a great match for managing a particular team no matter the capabilities and expertise, can negatively affect their effectiveness, reduce productivity and delay the achievement of organizational goals. What seems to matter most is the leader's ability to understand their own strengths and weaknesses and adapt their leadership style to suit the needs of their team and the organization they lead. Wise and effective leaders improve over time regardless of personality traits.

This is where the theories come in. They help leaders to accept and manage the varying personality traits and types and align the behaviors to who God intended them to serve.

As a Christian leader in a professional space, it is my firm belief that Christian leaders are strategically anointed, appointed and purposefully commissioned by God in top positions where our personality traits (good and bad) are needed to help the persons that need them to grow and change and help us to positively develop and mature. When I triangulate and integrate the data from all these theories, I have come to the following conclusions.

A sanguine personality type would likely be high on extraversion because of their friendly outgoing, pleasant and energetic personality.

Additionally, sanguine mostly settle or fall into the influencer behavioral style. This makes them some of the quickest to adapt to new ways of working (openness). They thrive through daily interactions, impromptu conversations and the wellbeing boost of socializing with colleagues, clients and customers.

Therefore, to successfully manage team members with a sanguine personality type, who is high on openness, leaders must never leave engagement to chance. Instead, you should provide numerous opportunities for them to build relationships and create outlets for social connection. Buddy systems, mentoring and coaching, celebrating team exploits and creating space for informal discussion will also reduce isolation and help to maximize productivity.

A choleric personality type (such as I) is more likely to be high on conscientiousness because they tend to be goal oriented and driven, highly active and busy. They are great multitaskers and they do not shy away from conflict and confrontation. They are also quick decision makers who love righting the wrongs of the world. They can be intolerant with procrastinators, blame gamers and persons who nurture a victim mentality. Thus, they are often viewed as impatient, curt and rude. They carry a confident persona and are more extroverted than introverted, although they often retreat into themselves for deep self-reflection.

It makes sense that they would settle or fall into

the dominance behavioral type. Persons with a dominance behavioral disposition want to get to the point, achieve results and attain rewards.

They do not respond well when you give commands and not provide the specific objectives and expectations for them to achieve organizational and personal goals. A very significant note is that they tend to become demotivated if they are micro-managed. Therefore, to successfully empower and effectively motivate team members who possess dominance behavioral type is to always strive to set both urgent and important goals and always communicate the big picture. Providing the right level of challenge, engagement and autonomy, whilst being alert to signs of stress and burnout are crucial and beneficial considerations for them to deliver and thrive.

A phlegmatic personality type is usually high on agreeableness because of their calm, patient, empathetic and easygoing nature. They are good at resolving conflict or smoothing ruffled feathers. However, they are mostly, indecisive and mostly shy away from making tough decisions. Their personality type and demonstrable personality traits mostly settle them in the compliance behavioral type. Leaders enhance the success of team members with a compliance behavioral type when they provide detailed updates, clearly define objectives and consistently reassure them. Additionally, assigning logical, analytical tasks and forwarding materials in advance of face-to-face meetings will allow you to get the most out of team members with this characteristic. It is very important that as a leader you sincerely, continuously and logically affirm and maintain the status quo as changing their work environment can feel chaotic for them.

Finally, the melancholy personality type is very high in the neuroticism category because they are emotionally sensitive, introverted and reserved, cautious but analytical and detailed oriented. They excel at planning and can have perfectionistic tendencies. For these reasons and more, they often settle into the steadiness behavioral type as they have a very low tolerance for stress and often find any change or new work environments challenging. They prefer to work remotely as they resent being disturbed, interrupted or confronted.

Leaders assist team members with a steadiness behavioral type to succeed by affording them the psychological safety to raise concerns, complimenting them, listening to them and modelling emotional intelligence. Most importantly, steadier types with a melancholic disposition prefer to listen than speak. Leaders can support them by providing environments that enhance their ability to concentrate and help them to structure their work to meet deadlines and increase productivity.

Personally, speaking this chapter holds the most benefits for beginning leaders, middle managers as well as leadership executives who want to overcome the relationship challenges as a Christian leader in a professional space. Your personality traits more often than not, influence how you lead for better or for worse.

The difference with Christian leaders is that God expect us to harness our personality traits to lead better and not worse. He places us in this position with a love note, " You have not chosen me, but I have chosen you and ordained you that you may go forth and bring forth fruit, fruit that we last, and whatever you ask in my name the Father will give you"- (John 15:16). He also gives us an important instruction ' see then that he walks circumspectly, not as fools but as wise redeeming the times' – (Eph. 5:15).

Thus, it is important that Christian leaders understand how to harness their personality traits to become more effective in their leadership.

The greatest thing about God is that he is fair and

just in his assessment of our character. He gives us personality traits that we need to overcome the situations and circumstances in our everyday life. He also allows us to possess and develop more than one, so we always have a spare trait to use in times of crisis.

As a Christian leader, you must know, acknowledge and examine your personality traits and preferences and surrender to God those that you have acquired by default. An objective analysis united with a divine influence will show you how you can re-wire those that are not enhancing you or those you serve. For example, how you can become less exacting and more empathetic.

Second, as a Christian leader, you must choose to use your personality traits to help and not hinder regardless of the situation. If you are great at helping people, help them even if they are ungrateful. If you are good at soothing ruffled feathers, do it even when you are being insulted. Own your strengths and giftings of your personality when God gives you opportunity to develop them. Your strengths are made perfect in trial and not in ease.

Third, use the right personality traits to complete what God has set you there to do which is to represent him and secure His glory. Recognize that you are the best pulse check to your team. Do not ignore the wisdom, feedback and constructive criticism from your team. Use it to develop and mature as a leader. "Show proper respect to everyone' –1 Peter 2:17). Finally, be transparent. You are human. Your personality traits can sometimes make you do the right thing in the wrong way. The key is to always try to treat others the way you want to be treated if the situation was reversed. Strive to be the leader that you would love to follow. "Be an example in word, in conversation, in charity, in spirit, in faith, in purity' – (1 Tim. 4:12).

As you ponder on this chapter as yourself these questions:

As a Christian leader how can I harness my personality traits to lead more effectively?

What does a healthy team dynamic look like to me? Am I the type of leader that I would follow?

Leadership Nugget

'The meeting of two personalities is like the contact of two chemical substances: if there is any reaction, both are transformed' - Carl Jung

Let us pray:

Dear God,

I pray for leadership guidance because being a leader is hard, but I know that through you, it can be done. Grant me discernment to identify the needs of my team through divine wisdom and understanding. Help me not be an ineffective leader, but to act for the betterment of Your Kingdom. Amen

Chapter 13

Equipped to Succeed

'Not by might nor by power, but by my Spirit says the Lord of hosts' – Zech. 4:6

If you are reading this book, and have gotten to this final chapter, you are indeed chosen by God. You accept and understand the necessity for you to be a leader driven by a God given purpose rather than position or power. You have asked and answered or is still getting the answer to the question 'Why did God choose me as a leader?

You have accepted that as a Christian leader you are a steward and a partner.

You realize that if serving is below your leadership is beyond you.

You have, or you are analyzing your levels of assignments, navigating your tests (wilderness experience) leadership pains and how each is connected to your divine mission and destiny.

You are clarifying your misconceptions of leadership, learning, and relearning your leadership roles and responsibilities and how your personality traits and style influence your leadership as a leader of excellence in your professional space.

Furthermore, you are reimagining how to motivate, empower, inspire and drive organizational goals in the fifth generation where wireless technology and artificial intelligence (AI) has the potential to change so many things.

In previous chapters, I have highlighted that as a Christian leader you are first anointed, next appointed and then purposefully commissioned to serve. God prepared a marvelous journey for you and he has a lot in store for you. He equips you by allowing you to learn on the job and gives you specific experiences to guide you if you are determined to reach your full potential.

I have presented my experiences starting with my leadership journey as a Christian leader serving in a global professional space, what I am today, what I went through and what I have learnt. I share my leadership story to turn on the light of hope and overcoming to let you know that as a Christian career professional you are not alone. I present my conclusions and offer practical suggestions and tips on how to harness your leadership superpower and become that leader; an overcomer.

Christian Leadership Facts

Your leadership appointment is not an accident, nor a mistake. Each of us as leaders bring unique gifts, talents, capabilities and abilities into this world. God places us in positions where we can use what we have to accomplish his purpose and do the most good. 'For we are God's handiwork, created in Christ Jesus to do good works, which God prepared in advance for us to do'- (Eph. 2:10). Ellen White says 'each of us has a mission of incredible importance that we cannot neglect or ignore. Your duty cannot be shifted upon another. No one but you can do your work. If you withhold your light, someone must be left in darkness through your neglect.

A purpose driven leader engages, empower, encourage and enlighten. However, purpose driven leadership does not equal instantaneous growth or change. It is gradual value-added transformation, rather than results orientation. Leaders and stakeholders can calculate the value that is added because its' build up equals systematic change.

I have learnt that systematic change takes time because it addresses mindsets, dispositions, filters, organizational culture, (formal and informal), policies, standards, guidelines and relationships. For systematic change to be successful, it must positively affect all persons on the results chain. The length of time or span of this change is solely dependent on who and what you are working with. Ellen White states that as a leader you' do not become a great stalwart overnight, God works on you, so you can work on people. God changes you, so you can change people'.

Your leadership appointment includes moments of great difficulty, but God makes provisions for you to overcome and be victorious at every twist and turn of the fight. 'No temptation has overtaken you that is not common to man. God is faithful, and he will not let you be tempted beyond your ability, but with the temptation he will also provide the way of escape, that you may be able to endure it' (1 Cor. 10:13).

The crisis of leadership is that we give lip service to leadership, but we do not practice it.

The heart of the crisis is that leadership has lost integrity. Accountability has become a dirty word that is used to reward 'leader performers' and 'slave catchers. It is now common knowledge that leaders are plentiful, but leadership is very scarce. We have far too many systems in place to evaluate leaders' performance, but we do not have any system in place for apprenticeship. It is my firm belief that apprenticeship must be integrated in leadership development. Strength comes from assimilation and practice. Apprenticeship addresses leadership on a personal level that allows you to grow into leadership as it moves you from speculation to revelation. The sad fact is that many leaders are too content to be a paralytic manager. Wheatley (2006) notes that all organizations need management and leadership, but leadership is particularly necessary to solve problems that do not have any easy answers.

As a l*eader, you must never confuse management with leadership.*

So many leaders have been caught in the leadership trap where they are cultured, trained and programmed to be primarily more task oriented which gradually evolved to be results oriented, rather than people oriented. This often results in capable managers who are of the mistaken conviction that they are effective leaders. They often find themselves more concerned with success primarily focused on achieving specific tasks, activities, processes, targets and goals that need to be accomplished.

They also tend to be more concerned with structure and adherence to procedure, managing processes and ensuring that tasks are completed quickly, efficiently and effectively. In the 'elevated' state of being namely 'results oriented', leaders are more concerned with the overall goals and outcomes of a project at an organizational level. They prioritize achieving the desired results and are often only willing to adapt or be flexible in their approach to achieve these results. I have found that the choice between task oriented and results oriented leadership depends on the leader, context, organization and the situation.

This should not be the case for Christian leaders in a professional space. Ellen White says 'it is not 'the capabilities that you now possess that will give you success, it is what the Lord can do for you. As Christian leaders, we need to have far less confidence in what man can do and less concerned about what they can't do, and far more confidence in what God can do'. Jesus warns us not to follow the manmade model or strategies but exemplify the servant leadership model and strategies of God. Personal accountability and self-discipline are at the heart of servant leadership. This is the only way to fulfill your leadership appointment and accomplish the purpose of your life on earth.

This is the only way to lead in the fullness of your potential. It is the process God designed for you to deny self, become his fruit bearer and a vessel of honor. Thus, as a Christian leader in a professional space you already carry a servant leadership model. You should be more concerned with significance that focuses primarily on serving, empowering and upskilling team members to focus on becoming first personally accountable, wise stewards and organizational partners.

This takes a little longer and prioritize a people-oriented approach because of the emphasis on compassion, care, kindness and service, which originated from our Christian teachings, core values and beliefs. However, this does not negate paying attention to the timely completion of tasks and the importance of results.

The main thing is that as a Christian leader you have a divine responsible to consider both tasks and results while also prioritizing the well-being and development of the people you have been chosen to lead.

As leaders in a professional space, we often become very busy trying to fulfill organizational goals, solve problems and keep pace with a rapidly changing workplace. It becomes so easy for them to lose focus amid the challenges, demands and programs. Christian leaders in your professional space are called to lead in a culture of change. You are God's instruments to bring people closer to him in an unwavering relationship, equip people for their work and to help them to remain focused on the mission of the organization. You are now equipped. You are now a wise leader.

Now that I understand and know that I as a Christian leader, I am equipped, I am wise, and I am not alone, the big question is;

How can I harness my leadership superpower to develop as a leader and make my organization more effective?

In this fifth-generation era with knowledge sharing and wireless technology, a wise leader should strive to be more collaborative than competitive. What I have learnt throughout my leadership journey and what I know is that there are some foundational steps that a wise Christian leader who serves in a professional space, should never miss or ignore.

Foundational Practices of a Wise Leader

A wise leader cultivates self-awareness

The first step towards harnessing your leadership superpower as a wise Christian leader is to develop self-awareness. 'For if a man think himself to be something, that ye is not, he deceives himself' – Gal. 6:3. Self-awareness is essential for a Christian leader in a professional space because it facilitates the integration of faith and leadership. It enables leaders to lead by example, make ethical decisions, communicate effectively, and foster a work environment that aligns with Christian values.

There are four main types of self-awareness: that is crucial for effective leadership. These include:

Internal self-awareness, which means that you are aware of your own thoughts, emotions, and values and understand your strengths, weaknesses, and motivations. The other is external self-awareness which involves being aware of how others perceive

you. It also involves understanding the impact of your behavior on others and being receptive to feedback.

Next, there is behavioral self-awareness in which you focus on recognizing and understanding your own behaviors and actions and understanding your habitual patterns and the triggers that influence your behavior.

The final one is relational self-awareness, which involves understanding your communication style, emotional reactions, and how you contribute to the dynamics of your relationships.

God wants us to examine ourselves as leaders- (2

Cor. 13:5). Self-awareness promotes self- control and help a leader to shape others, but a 'double minded man, is unstable in all his ways' – (James 1: 7-8). If you cannot control yourself, you can control nothing else. Self-awareness is the most important key to unlock leadership significance because it not only benefits the leader personality but also positively influences the team and the organization on a whole.

A wise leader creates a leadership cycle

Creating a leadership cycle also known as, a personal leadership development plan is crucial to ensure that as a leader you continue to grow and adapt to your organizational needs. The specific areas and components of a leadership cycle program varies according to the organization's needs, goals, culture and the level of leadership e.g. beginning, middle managers or executive.

It can also be a structured and ongoing initiative designed to cultivate and enhance the leadership skills and capabilities of the persons within your organization. 'Instruct the wise, and they will be even wiser. Teach the righteous, and they will learn even more'- (Prov. 9:9). The ultimate aim can be to develop a pipeline of capable leaders who can steer the organization toward its goals and adapt to a rapidly changing work environment.

These are the important elements that should not be left out of a leadership cycle program. These are strategic management, skill development, conflict resolution and negotiation, change management, group dynamics, leadership styles and models, team building and collaborating, feedback and evaluation.

A wise leader provides a clear vision and the vehicles that bring team members to their destination

It is a leader's responsibility to have a vision of a better future and a path to get there. Your main function is to inspire and get your team member to follow that vision. God knows that having and articulating your vision is important. He says, 'write the vision and make it plain, that he may run that reads it' Hab. 2:2.

You have to share your vision in such a compelling way that people are compelled to follow you. To get teammates to buy into and own your vision you have to actively listen to your team, facilitate open dialogue and ensure that information passes smoothly throughout your organization. When you are able to lovingly persuade and garner consensus, your teammates follow you because they want to be part of that future.

A wise leader develops a leadership strategy that can achieve your goals

Effective leadership strategies play a crucial role in promoting the growth and success of an organization. It involves making deliberate choices on how to lead, manage resources, make decisions, motivate, and inspire the members of the organization in your contexts and environment. It involves developing your own best practices.

A wise leader sets both urgent and important goals and specific objectives

Two often overlooked blockers of effective leadership is that leaders do not set both urgent and important goals and specific objectives and the other is that they sometimes change direction, expectations and objectives without communicating the new expectations to team members. When you fail to set both urgent and important goals, you force team members to decide what is urgent and what is important to them. Their important often ends up getting in the way of your organization's urgent.

Also, announcing a change of direction or goals without a clear and proper understanding
of what is to be accomplished by whom and when, often result in stagnation.

When you make it your point of duty to strike the well- needed balance between what is urgent and what is important and effectively communicate specific expectations, guidelines, instructions and roles, it will help you as a leader to have a bigger impact and avoid burnout. Moreover, it will ensure that your team members understand their roles and responsibilities. Thus, your teammates will be able to contribute in ways that are more meaningful without wasting resources.

A wise leader creates action plans

Personal and organizational action plans propel you forward. Developing a step-by-step detailed outline of the tasks, resources, funds and timelines required to accomplish the desired outcomes personally and professionally, is an excellent way to measure and monitor the value- added components and implement any adjustments needed. An action plan is a wise guide to make your path easier. Without knowledge, action is useless. Without action, knowledge is futile. Knowledge gives power only when you apply it.

A wise leader knows and appropriately uses leadership styles

In the previous chapter, I engaged in a detailed discussion with numerous examples showing how leadership styles, personality traits and behavioral styles intersect. Simply put leaders' help people grow.

Your leadership style usually fits into two categories hard vs soft or high vs low. The hard or low side usually attacks, criticizes, offends, hurt and alienates. The soft or high side usually defends, apologizes, trains, forgives and love.

According to Professor M. S. Rao, founder of MSR Leadership Consultants, there are several differences between soft and hard leadership. 'Soft leadership emphasizes persuasion while hard leadership emphasizes pressure; soft leadership focuses on transformation while hard leadership focuses on task; soft leadership emphasizes soft power while hard leadership pushes hard power; and soft leadership focuses on soft tactics while hard leadership focuses on hard tactics. He emphasizes that 'soft leaders adopt transformational, democratic, servant and authentic leadership styles while hard leaders adopt the transactional and autocratic styles of leadership. Soft leaders are others-centered leaders while hard leaders are often self-centered leaders.

More importantly, 'hard leaders work within the organizational culture while soft leaders change the organizational culture. Hard leaders think within the box while soft leaders think outside the box. Hard leaders are competitive, data- driven and short-term focused while soft leaders are creative, collaborative, organic and long-term focused. Hard leaders take people where they want them to go, while soft leaders take people voluntarily from where they do not necessarily want to go, but where they ought to be. Soft leaders do not force people to follow; they invite people on a journey. Soft leaders focus on strategies while hard leaders focus on processes.

He makes the very important point that in this fifth-generation era, 'your soft skills are what makes the difference and increase positive outcomes in the workplace, either as an employee or as a leader. As an employee, you learn to behave well as per the situation, needs and feelings of others, and as a leader, you get the tasks executed smoothly without inviting any troubles and ill will among your employees'.

It is his belief that 'soft leadership equips organizations with several advantages for achieving excellence and effectiveness'. Not only does it help to transform the personality, attitude and behavior of the people, it also balances people and task-orientation proportionately without compromising the organizational goals and objectives. It emphasizes empathy that is the heart of servant leadership. Leading with empathy refers to the leaders' 'ability to step into the shoes of teammates and look at the issues objectively to achieve the desired outcomes. The soft side is always preferred but a wise leader learn when to use each.

A wise leader delegate responsibly.

In the previous chapters, I explored the concept of delegation, and how we misunderstand delegation. A wise leader sets the tone for the team by drawing on its best assets. They choose persons whose actions match their words and who model integrity. Integrity is 'who you are'. Who you are is how you act. How you act is who you are'.

In the instance that you have to choose the best of the worse, assign tasks to team members based on their skills, strengths, and expertise.
Ensuring a fair distribution of workload and clear expectations. In addition, as they take on the new roles and responsibilities make sure to empower them.

Efficiently, allocate the relevant resources and reasonable timelines required to accomplish tasks and goals. If you support them, they will support you.

On a cautious note if you cannot trust them, do not appoint them. A lack of trust always results in micromanagement that can end in resentment, tension and strained relationships. Nonetheless, monitoring and evaluating the progress of tasks and projects allow you to identify potential bottlenecks or issues and taking corrective measures as needed.

A wise leader promotes continuous learning

As a leader, you must see to it that you are always improving and learning as a leader. 'Your growth determines who you are. Who you are determines who you will attract. Who you will attract determines the success of your organization'. A wise leader is supportive. As a wise leader you know that supporting your team is part of your job. You help your team members to grow and expand. You also help your team to self- examine. You promote and teach consistent and never-ending improvement. You help each team member become more, do more, produce, more and know more.

A wise leader works to build relationships

Strong relationships build strong teams. Strong teams build strong organizations. A wise leader knows that you influence the group with who you are. You understand the impact of ego on self and others. Ego is the false self that you defend. If you understand how your ego gets in your way, you will see how your ego gets in others' way.

You know how to quietly connect with others to create loyalty, but a poor leader shares credit generously. You practice or teach honesty, openness and willingness to act on the things that matter. You are aware of the organizational goals, processes, individual and groups and understand how these affect each other. This understanding drives you to do everything in your power to make things go smoother.

You have an agenda that is adaptable and purposeful. You quickly address challenges and obstacles that arise, analyzing the root cause and implementing solutions to keep the team on track. You continuously review and refine work processes to enhance efficiency, reduce waste and optimize resource utilization whilst negotiating them with a win-win attitude. You coordinate efforts across team members respecting their failures; handholding them; motivating them constantly; aligning their energies and efforts; and recognizing and appreciating their contributions in accomplishing organizational goals and objectives'.

A wise leader makes informed decisions

Most times the leader stands alone when tough decisions have to be made in an organization. The popular statement that experience teaches wisdom is personally applicable to me when it comes to decision making. I have had numerous light bulb and frustrating moments as an influential informed decision-maker. Although I always strive to be transparent, open, empathetic and kind, doing what I have to do and not how I feel, is sometimes highly traumatic as in instances like these you can never win. My tough decision moments have definitely taught me beneficial leadership lessons.

One very significant leadership lesson when involved in tough decision-making is that no amount of logic will motivate team members to make a tough decision, the buck stops with the leader.

Another is that force causes resistance. A wise leader needs to be patient and gentle when negotiating a tough decision realizing how important it is to coerce teammates rather than appear to work against them. This is the only alternative to force. 'A man convinced against his will is of the same opinion still'. Keep things simple and focused. A confused mind does not act. Being specific and clear help team members to understand and support change. Besides *a wise leader knows that you 'only win agreements not arguments.*

Making timely and well-informed decisions is always the ideal. However, there have been instances on my leadership journey when I did not have that luxury. In these instances, I have had to take the lonely road, being as positive as I can and be focused and purposeful.

I have learnt the philosophy of the 'bloodless coup' realizing that 'people will forget the good you do for them, but they will never forget the bad they do to you'. I have utilized the art of using relationship power over authority power on several occasions. For that reason, I always try to kill the monster while it is small. A wise man said' in the life of every problem, there comes a time when it is big enough to see, but small enough to deal with'. I have learned that 'The best victory is the victory won without striking a blow.' As a leader, never forget that what is not worked out will be acted out. Never let employees' complaints fester and never ignore the persistent complaints of one employee about another.

A wise leader rejuvenates and take rest or time for reflecting

There is a saying a man in a room by himself can solve most problems. A wise leader knows that stillness creates clarity, insight, creativity and strength. You cannot hear yourself if you are not listening. When you understand self, you can understand others. Taking time to reflect helps you to know what and who triggers you and how.

This deep reflection and observation help you to, identify, monitor and even eliminate your triggers. A wise leader also learns how to work smarter, not harder. On your leadership journey, take time to do the things that matter.

Never choose to die silently by consistently missing lunch, doctor's appointment and spending quality time with your family to meet deadlines. You just cannot put out what you do not put in and you cannot receive what you have not released. Besides, if you die tomorrow or when you leave, the organization goes on as if you had never been there.

Careful, honest, open self-reflection will amplify

your perspective on your personal and professional issues. Understand the need to lead with self-care and self-compassion. Understand the value of having mercy on yourself, because as a leader no one else does. . Remember he who fights and run away, lives to find another day.

Besides, as a Christian leader self-care is of utmost importance. You accept that 'your body is the temple of the Holy Spirit, you are not your own. Therefore, honor God with your body'- (1Cor. 6:19 - 20). You have a duty to take care of and honor your body. God want us 'to prosper while being in good health, (3 John 1:2). He leads us to use our body and our gifts to achieve the will of God.

A wise leader engages in career planning

Should Christian leaders prepare for the future? I say a resounding yes. Ignoring or facing the truth does not make it go away. The skills that carry you to this point are not necessarily the skills that will carry you on. A wise leader learns the skills you need to function for the next three to five yrs. You have to survive and position yourself as a leader in the upcoming environment. You should expect unprecedented and rapid changes. The dynamics of leadership is also changing and will eventually explode.

The presence of artificial intelligence (AI) is becoming more and more foreboding. You should never go into a battle unprepared. You have to be alert and sober and prepare and cultivate the skills that you will need. Change will teach you a hard lesson if you refuse to change. Upskilling and upscaling has become non-negotiables. In order not to be left behind, you have to adapt. You have to adjust your mindset.

As you read the last lines of this book, I have used this book to stimulate awareness, hope and turn on a bright light for Christian leaders serving in a professional space.

You have been illuminated. You voice, and service have been amplified. You are armed and ready. Your assignment, roles and responsibilities are much clearer. You are equipped. God says, 'Go forth' '

The world is waiting for a leader like you.

Leadership nugget

"The question isn't who is going to let me; it's who is going to stop me' Ayn Rand

Let us pray:

Dear God,

Thank you for entrusting me with the responsibility of leadership. You have equipped me to become a more effective and servant hearted leader. Help me to apply the knowledge and wisdom gained during the reading of this book. Thank you for the divine training that I have received. Equip me to lead with integrity, humility, and a heart for others. Thank You for the opportunity to grow as a leader. Amen

APPENDIX A

Guiding Principles for effective Christian leadership in a professional space

As leaders, it is important to regularly reflect on your roles, actions, and decisions. Here are some questions that you can ask yourself to promote self-awareness, personal growth, and effective leadership. It is essential to be honest with yourself and use your answers to identify areas for improvement and act accordingly.

➢ Am I leading by example?

Do my various actions align with the values and principles I expect from my team?

➢ Am I effectively communicating with my team?

Are my expectations clear and am I actively listening to them concerns and feedback?

➢ Am I providing a supportive and inclusive environment for my team

➢ Do I encourage my team members and encourage their professional growth?

➢ Am I delegating responsibilities and trusting them to achieve their goals?

➢ Am I fostering a positive and motivating work culture?

➢ Do I recognize and appreciate the achievements and contributions of my team members?

➢ Am I open to new ideas and perspectives

➢ Do I actively seek and value the input of my team members?

➢ Am a making decision based on emotion, speculation or association?

➢ Am I considering the potential impact of my decisions on various stakeholders?

➢ Am I adaptable and open to change?

➢ Do I embrace innovation and encourage my team to think creatively?

➢ Am I managing conflicts and challenges effectively?

➢ Am I taking care of my own well- being?

Do I prioritize self-care, manage my stress levels and seek? personal growth opportunities?

APPENDIX B

Personal Checklist for a Christian Career Professional

✓ I consult God every day for direction and guidance

✓ I put aside personal time each day to spend with God, my family and myself.

✓ I lead with compassion, kindness, fairness, transparency and integrity.

✓ I empower everyone individually but equally to become his/her best self.

✓ I use facts and logic rather than emotion, association and peer pressure to make organizational decisions.

✓ I do what is right not what is popular

✓ I seek God's favor and knowledge in all my efforts.

APPENDIX C

Leadership Commandments for Beginning Leaders

The greatest thing that can come between you and your success is false pride.

'An arrogant, conceited or haughty leader will make costly mistakes, but a humble and modest leader will clearly see right and wrong, truth and error, wisdom and folly' – Psa. 11:2

Here are five leadership commandments to overcome false pride.

> P – Don't be entangled by your position that you disregard people. Leadership need people.

> R – Never allow your passion, feelings or emotions to rule you, especially when making decisions. Act as you must not as you feel. Act as you must not as you feel.

> I – Never be insensitive to or ignore individuals' feelings or needs to meet your organizational goals. Persons need to know that you care about them as much as you care about meeting your goals.

> D – Never let your achievements dazzle you. Overcome your success. You can't progress if you keep looking at your trophies instead of future goals. forward is forward.

➢ E – Never think you know everything because you know so many things. if you stop growing you should not be leading. Great leaders have a teachable spirit.

APPENDIX D

Leadership commandments for Christian leaders in a professional space

I am sharing the Christian leadership commandments that have provided guidance and direction throughout my leadership journey. It is always a good practice to create your own.

Commandment #1: Always put your relationship with god first.

Commandment#2: Always be honest, just, fair and transparent with yourself and others.

Commandment #3: Always pray for wisdom and discernment in making decisions and leading your team.

Commandment #4: Always love and treat your neighbor, as you would want to be treated.

Commandment #5 Always be a servant leader. Serve others with a humble heart and be patient when dealing with challenges.

Commandment #6: Always pray for your team's success, well-being and spiritual growth.

Commandment #7: Always take responsibility for the resources and talents entrusted to you and use them wisely for the benefit of others.

Commandment#8: Always trust in God's plan and timing even when facing challenges or uncertainties.

Commandment#9: Always lead by example and serve the needs of your team just as Jesu served His examples.

Commandment#10: Always uphold a high standard of honesty and ethical behavior in all your dealings.

APPENDIX E

Leadership Development Program Curriculum

Program Objectives: Develop leadership skills and competencies in participants.

Foster a culture of effective, ethical, inclusive servant leadership Prepare participants to lead and influence teams, projects.

Curriculum Components:

Module 1: Introduction to Leadership
- Understanding Leadership Appointment
- Leadership Management
- Understanding Leadership Styles
- The Role of Emotional Intelligence, Growth Mindset, Kindness and Empathy

Module 2: Communication and Influence
- Developing Effective Communication Skills
- Building Credibility and Trust
- Understanding Leadership Influence
- Influencing Skills

Module 3: Decision Making and Problem Solving
- Decision making Models
- Critical Thinking
- Problem solving Techniques

Module 4: Team Building and Collaboration
- Team Dynamics and Team Development Stages
- Conflict Resolution and Negotiation
- Building High- Performing Teams

Module 5: Servant Leadership
- Authentic Leadership vs Moral Leadership
- Values –based Leadership vs Leading with Integrity
- Ethical Leadership and Values
- Ethical Decision Making

Module 6: Change Management
- Adapting to Change
- Leading Change Initiatives
- Overcoming Resistance to Change

Module 7: Leadership in Times of Crisis
- Understanding Crisis Levels
- Leading During Crisis
- Resilience and Crisis Management
- Communication in Crisis Situations

Module 8: Leadership in a Global Context
- Cultural Sensitivity and Global Leadership
- Leading International Teams
- Cross-Cultural Communication

Module 9: Diversity, Equity and Inclusion
- Understanding Unconscious Bias
- Promoting Diversity and Inclusion
- Creating an Inclusive Work Environment

Module 10: Leadership Project
- Participants work on a leadership project or case study
- Applying leadership concepts to real – world situations
- Project presentations and peer evaluations

Module 11: Mentoring and Coaching
- Pairing participants with mentors or coaches
- Individualized guidance and support

Module 12: Leadership Reflection and Feedback
- Participants reflect on their leadership journey
- Gathering feedback from peers and mentors
- Setting personal and professional leadership goals

Graduation and Certification Upon successful completion of the program, participants receive a leadership development certificate.

NB. In practice, leadership curricula can be highly customized to address the unique needs and goals of the organization and may vary in length and complexity.

Leadership Training

One – Month Christian Leaders Training Program

A one-month Christian leadership training program for beginning leaders in a professional space is a condensed but intensive and focused curriculum aimed at emphasizing the effective integration of leadership skills, ethical principles and Christian values.

Three – Month Christian Leaders Training Program

A three-month leadership-training program for Christian leaders in a professional space combines spiritual and leadership development emphasizing Christian principles of servant leadership, ethics, and integrity. It aims to equip career professionals with the tools they need to be effective leaders while also fostering spiritual growth and a deeper connection with their faith.

Six Months /One Year Christian Leaders Training Program

A six months /one-year training program for Christian leaders in middle management and executive positions or beginning leaders in a professional space is a comprehensive curriculum designed to equip beginning and experienced professionals with advanced leadership skills, integrate Christian values into their leadership roles, and foster personal and spiritual growth.

Book your FREE 15mins Life Coaching or Leadership Empowerment Session @http://calendly.com/drtpmotivateme2/30min and ASK ME ANYTHING

Register for your Leadership Training/ Life Coaching

Program: 1:1 Coaching   Group Coaching

@drtpmotivateme2@gmail.com

OR

@drtpmotivate2.com

I am Dr. Marcia Thomas your transformation partner. Changing lives. Changing outcomes. Together we overcome.